# From Hurt
# to Hope

of related interest

**Supporting Autistic People with Eating Disorders**
A Guide to Adapting Treatment and Supporting Recovery
*Edited by Kate Tchanturia*
ISBN 978 1 78775 445 4
eISBN 978 1 78775 446 1

**A Clinician's Guide to Mental Health Conditions
in Adults with Autism Spectrum Disorders**
Assessment and Interventions
*Edited by Eddie Chaplin, Debbie Spain and Jane McCarthy*
ISBN 978 1 78592 426 2
eISBN 978 1 78450 800 5

**Living with PTSD on the Autism Spectrum**
Insightful Analysis with Practical Applications
*Lisa Morgan, MEd and Mary P. Donahue, PhD*
*Foreword by Tony Attwood*
ISBN 978 1 78775 050 0
eISBN 978 1 78775 085 2

**A Practical Guide to Happiness in
Adults on the Autism Spectrum**
A Positive Psychology Approach
*Victoria Honeybourne*
ISBN 978 1 78592 577 1
eISBN 978 1 78450 988 0

**A Guide to Mental Health Issues in Girls and
Young Women on the Autism Spectrum**
Diagnosis, Intervention and Family Support
*Dr Judy Eaton*
ISBN 978 1 78592 092 9
eISBN 978 1 78450 355 0

# From Hurt to Hope

## Stories of Mental Health, Mental Illness and Being Autistic

EDITED BY MAIR ELLIOTT

**Jessica Kingsley Publishers**
London and Philadelphia

First published in Great Britain in 2022 by Jessica Kingsley Publishers
An Hachette Company
2
Copyright © Jessica Kingsley Publishers 2022

The information contained in this book is not intended to replace the services
of trained medical professionals or to be a substitute for medical advice.
The complementary therapy described in this book may not be suitable for
everyone to follow. You are advised to consult a doctor before embarking on any
complementary therapy programme and on any matters relating to your health, and
in particular on any matters that may require diagnosis or medical attention.

Trigger warning: This book mentions abuse, alcohol, anxiety,
self-harm, eating disorders and trauma.

A CIP catalogue record for this title is available from the
British Library and the Library of Congress

ISBN 978 1 78775 585 7
eISBN 978 1 78775 586 4

Printed and bound in Great Britain by Clays Ltd

Jessica Kingsley Publishers' policy is to use papers that are natural, renewable and recyclable
products and made from wood grown in sustainable forests. The logging and manufacturing
processes are expected to conform to the environmental regulations of the country of origin.

Jessica Kingsley Publishers
Carmelite House
50 Victoria Embankment
London EC4Y 0DZ

www.jkp.com

*To those who Helped me through my Hurt
and gave me the opportunity to find Hope.*

*My dearest family, Beth, Antonia, Lizzie, Tanya, Mrs Tomlin,
Mrs Gregson, Mrs Phillips and many more.*

# Contents

Introduction   9

**Who Am I?**   28
*Mair Elliott*

**I Don't Really Wanna Fight No More**   57
*Morénike Giwa Onaiwu*

**Hurting, Helping and Hoping: From Learning to Diagnosis and Contentment**   70
*Paul Statham*

**Feeling Alien in a World That Rejects You: The Discovery of Self Through Neurodiversity**   95
*Suzy Rowland*

**To Be Left Alone**   115
*Emma Wishart*

**Being Autistic and Managing Anxiety**   133
*Robert Joyce*

**Hoyo (Mum) and Inankeedii's (Son) Journey from Hurt to Hope with Autism**   154
*Nura Aabe*

**Big Brain Trees and Superpowers: A Journey of Discovery, Patience and Understanding**          160

*Emma Cobb*

**My Journey to a Place of Hope: Autism and Schizophrenia**          179

*Yenn Purkis*

**A Particle of My Existence**          190

*Casey Chonily*

**Thriving Through Words: Finding Your Niche in a Neurotypical World**          212

*Jess/Jai White*

Conclusion          216

About the Authors          226

Endnotes          230

# Introduction

Dear reader, may I take the opportunity to give you some background information before you go on to read the poignant stories that lie ahead in this book?

I started this project with the naive thought that it would be easy. Over the year in which I have been running this project, I have laughed, cried, screamed and raged. I have done a lot of campaign work, and I have worked with many people and organizations, but perhaps this project really hit home the difficulty of straddling both sides of the argument. I am autistic and a keen supporter of progressive societal change to end the injustices experienced by the neurodivergent, disabled and others. But I am also part of the 'institution' because of the organizations I have worked with and for. I understand and represent both sides – that society needs to change, and that change takes time. I have tried to walk the tightrope to please both parties. I have, as always, trusted my gut and done what I thought to be right.

While in discussion with the publishers I suggested including as many different autistic voices as I could. Since my autism diagnosis I have found solace, relief, camaraderie, humour, annoyance and more in the online autism community. The community has helped me understand myself as an autistic person, supported me in my darkest hours and celebrated with me during triumphs, large or small. I know and feel the power of belonging to a community that understands you. I wanted to take a small piece of that and put it into a book.

The instructions given to each author were to write an essay based on personal experiences of autism and mental health/mental illness/mental health difficulties. These essays needed to cover the topics of hurt (the authors' experiences and how they felt), help (what has helped them) and hope (what gives them hope). Finally, I emphasized the need to express the human nuances of their experiences, to counter the dominant clinical view of autism.

The essays submitted were beyond what I could have hoped for. Touching, heart-wrenching, humorous, anger-inducing, informative, challenging and more. I wish I could have accepted all submissions. In the end, I had to make tough choices and pick the essays most suitable for this project. I would like to thank everyone who expressed an interest and/or submitted an essay.

Ten contributors were chosen to be included, and over the collection many topics are explored. But first, perhaps I should briefly explain autism in case you are new to the field. Autism is a neurodevelopmental 'disorder' characterized by communication and sensory differences. Autism affects how a person perceives and interacts with the world around them. Roughly 1 in 160 people are autistic worldwide.[1] It is a spectrum condition with a wide variation between individual autistic people in how their autism affects them.

Most clinical texts about autism will use medical language and will suggest deficiency, disorder and, generally, a lack of humanness. However, many of us subscribe to a different way of describing ourselves. Neurodiversity, a concept coined by J. Singer in 1998,[2] explains autism as a difference not a defect, a much-needed variation in the population in how people engage and interact with the world. However, living in a world designed for a different kind of brain brings its challenges; many of us struggle with the sensory onslaught of modern life, we are often ostracized or misunderstood due to our alternative ways of communicating, and we are frequently unable to access basic services and infrastructure in order to live our lives with maximum health and happiness. I will expand on this a little further later on.

The term 'neurodiverse' refers to all people; 'neurodivergent' refers to those who have neurological difference, such as autism, attention deficit hyperactivity disorder (ADHD) and learning disabilities. 'Neurotypical' is the term describing all people who are not neurodivergent. You may have come across other terms as well, such as high functioning and low functioning, Asperger's syndrome and 'the spectrum'. All are references to autism; some are references to specific groups of autistic people. High-functioning autism and Asperger's syndrome refer to people who are autistic and society deems to be most able to live relatively 'normally'. Low-functioning autism refers to autistic people society deems to be least able to live 'normal' lives. Now I must stress that these assumptions are made in the context of a specific way of understanding what 'normal' is and a very specific societal structure. These are also assumptions that are predominantly made by neurotypical people. Autistic people tend not to like using functioning labels to describe themselves because autism isn't as simple as two polar opposite 'morphs'. To give an example, I have a friend who, like me, has been able to gain employment, has sat on many different boards and committees, has done a lot of public speaking, has competed at a high level in sport, and is capable and ready to move into independent living. I am considered to be 'high functioning', he is considered to be 'low functioning'. We are not polar opposites though, but the functioning labels suggest we are. What is worse, he may be prevented from realizing his potential because the system assumes that due to his functioning label he cannot achieve, and I may not get the support I need because it is assumed from my functioning label that I can cope.

Asperger's syndrome is generally considered to be a defunct term now. There is a history behind the term that I do not have the time or space to expand on here. Your unofficial homework is to research Hans Asperger and the history of Asperger's syndrome. Some still prefer to use 'Asperger's' to refer to themselves, however. 'The spectrum' is a better way of understanding autism comparable to functioning labels, although personally I have a weird relationship with the term and concept. My issue is that people seem to have decided that 'autism' is a dirty word and have taken to saying 'on the spectrum' when referring to autistic people. The word 'autism' is not a dirty word, and while we are at it, neither is 'autistic', 'disability' or 'disabled'.

While neurodivergent people struggle to live happy and healthy lives, that does not mean we are talentless, skill-less, have lesser worth than neurotypicals, and are unable to contribute to society in a meaningful way. There are many stereotypes out there about us, but perhaps the most toxic is that it is the autism itself that makes us incapable of leading happy and healthy lives. We live in societies which value very specific things – an ability to gain employment, for example – while simultaneously making those specific things inaccessible to anyone who is different. To expand on the employment example, many autistic people cannot gain employment because employers and workspaces are often actively damaging psychologically and do not allow neurodivergent people to flourish. If the ability to be employed is how we value people, then we automatically introduce the idea that those who are unable to access employment are of lesser value. This is despite the fact that if employment is made accessible, many of us could work and want to work. We could and should be able to lead healthy and normal lives, first by making society accessible to all, and second by changing how we see value in ourselves and other people.

A more clinical approach to autism might say that the neurodivergent person themselves needs fixing, that if the neurodivergent person could 'overcome' their 'disorder', then they would be able to have some value in society. Many people around the world choose to pursue this avenue. Frankly, most of the people I have met who choose to follow this belief are neurotypical professionals and carers. If I could have a penny for every time a neurotypical white man tried to explain autism to me using medical language, I would at least be able to afford my own house. Cure talk comes from this premise; that if the person could be liberated from their autism, they could become neurotypical. Many of us who are autistic or otherwise neurodivergent find this belief system to be deeply hurtful, traumatic and insulting. I can only speak for myself here, but 'curing my autism' would entail changing who I am as a person, i.e. I would no longer be myself if I was not autistic.

However, neurodivergence often comes along with unwanted and challenging co-morbid conditions, such as epilepsy,[3] gastro-intestinal problems,[4] Ehlers-Danlos syndrome,[5] mental health conditions[6] and many more. Autistic people's mental health has increasingly been under the lens, in the autism community itself, but also within professional fields, such as research and healthcare. This leads me to the topics within this book.

## Mental health

As you may be aware, mental health is quite a complex thing. Many factors contribute to our mental health, including bio-socio-economic factors. Each individual person will experience different factors that challenge or boost their mental health. The contributors to this book have covered a vast array of different topics, many of which I cannot go into full detail here in this introduction (the limiting factor of word counts!). However, I will try to give you a flavour of background information to the important topics.

Most, if not all, autistic people I have ever met have had some kind of history of psychiatric diagnoses; 79 per cent have co-occurring mental illness.[6] The most common psychiatric diagnoses given to autistic people are clinical depression and anxiety disorders. Here are some key statistics:

- Five in ten autistic adults have depression.[6]

- Nearly a third of autistic adults have a current anxiety disorder diagnosis.[7]

- Forty-two per cent of autistic children have diagnosed anxiety disorders.[8]

Other mental health conditions that are also frequent include anorexia nervosa,[9] obsessive compulsive disorder,[10] borderline personality disorder[11] and psychosis/schizophrenia.[12] There may be a biological underpinning making autistic people more susceptible to developing mental health disorders,[13] which would at least partly explain why so many of us struggle with our mental health. I think, however, the socio-economic factors cannot be underestimated. We face many challenges, including struggling in, or being kicked out of, education settings,[14,15] and being unable to get work and remain in employment.[16] We are often not in suitable housing or not the housing we want to live in,[17] we are forced to live off the meagre scrapings of benefits, those who require a high level of support are often not in control of their own lives, healthcare is not accessible to us,[18] we are isolated and often lonely,[19] and most iterations of society are not open to us. These factors play a huge role in the mental health of autistic people, a much larger role, I believe, than any genetic predisposition.

## Healthcare

While many of us struggle with our mental health, access to mental health care is woeful. One of three things usually happens when an autistic person attempts to access care for their mental health: 1) they get told that because they're autistic the service cannot help them; 2) the service says they can help them but no therapy within the service is appropriate or adapted to autistic people and therefore it is pointless, so the autistic person eventually gets discharged on the grounds that they are 'not engaging' or are 'untreatable'; or 3) the autistic person gets thrown around the system accruing diagnoses that are neither helpful nor correct and developing trauma from the system itself. Many people may experience all three at different times in their lives. All these three scenarios are also predicated on the fact that the person has an autism diagnosis. Many autistic people are not diagnosed, however. In this instance, their journey to get help is difficult to summarize. I can only say that in the times I have been stuck in psychiatric hospitals, many of my fellow inpatients were clearly undiagnosed autistic people – at one point I would say that out of five women in one unit, four of us were autistic, but besides me, the other three women had not been diagnosed. My attempts to notify doctors of this was met with disdain – doctors don't like it when their patients tell them what to do (at least in my experience anyway). If you are under any illusion that what I am saying is not true then I'd like to point out that on average autistic people have a life expectancy 16 years lower than neurotypical people, with suicide being the second biggest killer (behind heart disease) of autistic people without learning disability.[20,21]

Zooming out of a mental health specific focus, healthcare in general is inaccessible to autistic people also. Autistic people are at a higher risk of dying prematurely from almost every cause of death in comparison to neurotypical people. Epilepsy and heart disease[20,21] are two of the highest causes of premature death in autistic people. Shockingly, autistic people with learning disability are dying 30 years younger than neurotypical people.[20,21] Access to healthcare is not equal – autistic people of all support needs are dying younger than they should because of this.

## Trauma

Trauma is not something that has been researched enough in the autism community.[22] I'm not sure that even the autism community itself recognizes the overbearing trauma that exists in our lives as individual people and as a community. It's as if we've become used to breathing in the thick smog of trauma that envelops us. We have endured ages of mistreatment and abuse. It really isn't that long ago that we would have all been in lifelong institutions with no liberty or dignity. Some still remain in such barbaric – perhaps even more so – institutions in the UK, now with the fancy new name of 'assessment and treatment units' to distract the public from the human rights abuses that happen within those walls.[23] I have not met a single autistic person who cannot recall the earth-shattering experiences of being bullied and/or having to act 'normal' every day to avoid being bullied. I have not met a single autistic person who could tell me that they have been able to access education, employment, healthcare, housing and other basic rights, without immense and unreasonable stress. We have individual and collective trauma that colours who we are, how we engage with each other and how we engage with the world around us.

One fact that doesn't ever leave my brain is that autistic adults without learning disability are nine times more likely to die from suicide compared to the average population.[20,21] Even worse still, autistic children are 28 times more likely to consider suicide compared to non-autistic peers.[24] Perhaps what is most disturbing about these statistics is that they don't surprise me. My experiences have made me used to the idea that my peers, and myself, at some points, are in so much despair that death is an option many of us choose.

## Masking and camouflaging

The stories included in this book cover the topics of mental health diagnoses, anxiety, trauma, and suicide, as well as the inaccessibility of the neurotypical world. Given the premise of this book that shouldn't be surprising. Other more subtle topics are also discussed, such as masking and camouflaging.[25] Masking and camouflaging are the processes of concealing one's autism-ness and forcing oneself to appear neurotypical. This is a process that has mostly been associated with women and girls, but we need to move away from the binary way of understanding gender. Many boys, men, non-binary people and transgender people also mask and camouflage. It is one of the reasons why some of us don't get diagnosed until we are older – that and outrageously biased diagnostic tools.[26,27] It requires immense amounts of energy to perform such complex and intricate acts; the burden of doing it is often actively harmful to the autistic person's health. Despite it being a tool to be able to access the neurotypical world, the benefits often do not outweigh the negatives. A recent study found that autistic people who mask and camouflage their autism are more likely to experience suicidality.[28]

## Relationships

Relationships are also explored by some contributors, something which I was keen to include in the book. Often people seem to have the idea that autistic people are not capable of being in relationships, and as such are not exposed to both good relationships and unhealthy relationships. We are still human beings who have the same drives for intimacy and connection. We still fall into the traps of unhealthy, and sometimes abusive, relationships. We are mothers, fathers, daughters, sons, wives, husbands, partners. We are not islands, isolated from human nature. Although as I say this, I am probably not the person to be introducing this topic. I love my family and friends, but I am a very happy and resolute single person. The idea of being in a romantic relationship feels claustrophobic to me, and therefore I aim to grow old and turn into a crazy cat-lady – I am already part-way there. I am not the norm in the autism community though, and the world needs to wake up to the idea that love, connection and intimacy are not conditional to one being 'normal'.

## Carers

There has always been a divide between autistic people and carers, and perhaps this is most evident in the online community. It is a divide based on the premise that for years the voices of carers were often valued and listened to above the voices of the autistic people themselves. Society rang with the voices of onlookers; 'look at those poor people with the not-normal child, I bet they wished they had a normal child'. Desperate parents tried to force their children to be normal by applying barbaric and traumatizing therapies, equivalent to therapies designed to make gay people straight. Some were so ashamed of their autistic children they would voluntarily feed their child bleach when touted as a 'miracle cure' (it is not a miracle cure, it is poison). So rather than accept and love their autistic child some would prefer to poison and potentially kill their child. Even worse still, society then pitied the parents and not the child! I certainly look at the desperation of parents to make their autistic child normal as extremely hurtful. I can't help but be emotional about it; I am not a disaster. I am a person deserving of love and life as I am. For carers to not see that, the people who are supposed to be the source of infinite love and care, is upsetting. Autistic people are no longer shut away, hidden out of embarrassment, and thus the divide has become evident. We have platforms to speak on behalf of ourselves now, and we are not accepting this way of treating us anymore.

I am not saying that most carers do not love their children. I am not saying that most carers do not want the best for the person they care for. I am saying it is time that we moved on, moved away from old ways of thinking. Carers are part of the solution. I have met wonderful people who are carers over the years, people who are able to work with the autism community for progressive change. If we work together, we can get change for both autistic people and carers alike. I have included the stories of a couple of carers in this book because I think that the mental health of carers falls under the same banner as the mental health of autistic people. If those caring for us are unhappy and unhealthy, then how can we hope to be happy and healthy? If we can sing from the same hymn sheet, then there is hope for everyone. We are already part-way there on this journey to unite carers and autistic people, but more needs to be done.

## Intersectionality

As you read you will notice that I have crafted this book to include stories from a diverse group of people, although I will be the first to put my hand up and recognize that there are groups of people that are not represented here. I would like to have included a story from a non-speaking autistic person, but my deadline for delivery arrived before I could find someone who would be willing to share their story. Despite this, I hope that the range of voices offers you an idea of the diversity within the autism community – the community is much more than just white men. I will not shy away from the fact that racism exists within the community though. Autistic people of colour voice this every day. I have seen some in the community argue that autism is a 'get-out-of-jail-free' card when it comes to discussing race and racism. My short and simple answer to that is: NO, it is not. As autistic people, we are just as accountable for our actions, words and beliefs as anyone else in society. Being autistic does not mean we cannot challenge ourselves to understand, explore and vanquish our prejudices. Even if we do not recognize ourselves as racist, all white people need to put in the work to at least understand our privilege.

Having one or more 'underprivileges' does not mean we do not have other privileges. I may be autistic, which brings challenges, but I am also white, middle class and cisgender, which bring immense privileges. I benefit from a system that oppresses and disadvantages others. I may not like it, I certainly want to change it, but shying away from it won't help anyone. I am also privileged in that I am a speaking autistic person most of the time. I am able to voice my opinion. I am able to partake in a society that is heavily reliant on verbal communication. Some of my autistic peers do not have this privilege, and as a consequence their opinions, beliefs and thoughts are not heard and understood often enough. In this case, what we normally hear are others, often carers, speaking on their behalf, which is not the same as hearing the person themselves (no matter how well the carers think they know the person). I use the term 'hear' to mean more than just using our ears because communication is a term that covers a vast array of styles and modes.

The institutions that we battle every day as autistic people are doubly discriminating when it comes to black, indigenous, Asian, Latinx and other people of colour. These people are not only fighting a system biased against them as autistic people but also biased against them as non-white people. Just as it is within other areas, black people in particular are less likely to get an autism diagnosis compared to white people; instead, they are more likely to be given a conduct disorder diagnosis.[29,30] As a community we must ensure that in attempting to dismantle institutions which do not serve us our basic rights as autistic people, institutional racism is also dismantled.

We must also consider LGBTQIA+ (lesbian, gay, bisexual,

transgender, queer, intersex, asexual and others) people and anyone else who doesn't identify as straight and cisgender. Autistic people are just as diverse in gender and sexuality as the rest of society – I would even propose that autistic people are less likely than neurotypical people to conform to traditional binary gender stereotypes and heteronormativity (this is my impression and not a fact). Transphobia and homophobia are alive and present – a very real threat to the safety and well-being of neurodivergent and neurotypical LGBTQIA+ people alike. Within our community, we must ensure that we fight for their safety.

Intersectionality was a concept developed by Kimberlé Crenshaw[31] within the context of feminism, antiracist politics and black women. However, it quickly became a useful term in other contexts. Under the Oxford English Dictionary[32] 'intersectionality' is described as: 'The interconnected nature of social categorizations such as race, class, and gender, regarded as creating overlapping and interdependent systems of discrimination or disadvantage.'

Taking an intersectional understanding to neurodiversity offers a way to understand and dismantle societal structures and practices that disadvantage all people, not just a particular group. As Jewish American poet Emma Lazarus[33] wrote, 'Until we are all free, we are none of us free.'

I truly believe that working towards an autism community that has an intersectional mindset will influence more change in society to make the world accessible to more people. As for this book, I am not perfect, but I am trying to do my best and use the privilege I have responsibly. I hope this book reflects that.

## What does help look like?

Traditionally, help for mental health difficulties would be medication and talking therapy. Many of the contributors discuss their experiences with both of these tools. When adapted for autistic people, talking therapy is incredibly beneficial and important. Having a safe space to discuss and understand ourselves and our experiences within the context of the neurotypical world offers us a way of healing. Particularly as many of us have such low self-esteem and low self-worth, therapy adapted for us can assist in creating a much healthier and happier sense of self (the caveat being therapy not adapted for autistic people can often be damaging when applied to autistic people). However, the 'talking' part of 'talking therapies' makes these tools for addressing mental health problems inaccessible to many autistic people. Research is being done to adapt talking therapies for autistic people, and soon there will be options for us to access therapy that works for us.

I have a difficult relationship with medication which colours my view, but I know many autistic people who swear by it. It can take a lot of trial and error to find a type of medication, and the right dose, that works for you. Interestingly, many autistic people say that standard prescribed doses are too high, and taking half, even a quarter, of the lowest dose prescribed works for them – I am not aware of any research into the sensitivity of autistic people to psychiatric medication though, so this is only anecdotal. I suggest consulting with a doctor before making any changes to your medication.

The contributors to this book also discuss alternative forms of therapy, including various forms of art therapy. Art therapy may be more accessible to some autistic people, as the mode of communication is not so heavily reliant on speaking. Art, whether that be painting, writing, drama and so on, can offer a less confrontational way of exploring feelings and thoughts than traditional talking therapies. I know for myself that if I cannot give vocal descriptions of a feeling or thought, then painting or writing about it can offer a way of exploring what's going on. I must point out that art therapy will not suit everyone but may offer some a reasonable alternative to talking therapies.

Many autistic people I am familiar with often speak of how nature and animals help them cope. I have been lucky enough to have had a wide range of pets over the years, and they have played an enormous role in how I have coped with the world around me. I can't speak for anyone else, but I find that animals give me a sense of calm. I understand them. I do not feel as if I am missing crucial information when I am around animals, I can connect to them and develop a relationship without having to worry about jumping through the neurotypical social hoops. I am also lucky enough to live in a very rural part of the world. Nature surrounds me and keeps me grounded. Many of the contributors discuss their relationship with nature and have put it more eloquently than I could here. Sometimes I wonder if industrialization and urbanization were really worth it – I certainly could never live or spend more than a week in a city away from the green hills and crashing seas of my home. The sensory aspect of nature permeates into my mind and body, settling every sinew of stress and strain. I know that many of my peers feel the same way about nature.

There is a journey I see in a lot of people with autism. Maybe it is not exactly the same in all, but the general pattern is similar. Many begin their lives in chaos and turmoil, even despair, and the education system has a lot to answer for in this respect. Then there is a phase of unknowing and undoing. It's a phase of not knowing who we are, what we are about or what is going on in the neurotypical world. In this phase, many undo parts of who they truly are in order to fit into a world that is cruel and harsh. A tipping point is eventually reached and we, for whatever reason, begin to question why we are feeling so lost. From this point, we begin this steady journey which eventually culminates in accepting and embracing who we truly are. It begins with a gradual familiarization with our own needs.

Looking after oneself is hard. For autistic people who experience such dramatic and difficult barriers to our basic rights, it becomes ten times harder. When we start to familiarize ourselves with our needs, we are building pathways to a more authentic sense of self. We begin to understand who we are and what we are about. We start to be able to prioritize our needs above other demands. Many of the contributors to this book have phrased this in their own ways. Our needs come in varying levels and sizes, from the practical to the spiritual. Stimming is an example of a need we have as autistic people. For so long we have been told things like 'quiet hands!', 'stop fidgeting!' and 'sit still!', all ways of getting us to suppress our stims, to suppress our way of expressing ourselves, coping and regulating. As we break free from old ways of oppressing us, we are rediscovering stimming as a powerful tool at our disposal. Other needs for routine, repetition, quiet spaces, accommodations in education and employment, augmentative and alternative communication machines, and more, become apparent to us as we learn to reject the way in which we have been told we must behave to fit in with the neurotypicals.

When we reach a place in which we are more able to look after ourselves, a period of reflection often follows. This is a time for re-evaluating our experiences and the traumas we have been through. Understanding our trauma and how it has impacted us changes how we view ourselves. Many if not all of the contributors' stories in this book include some kind of trauma, whether it is grief, domestic abuse, bullying, traumatic environments, institutional trauma, or the trauma of living in a world that simply does not work for us. Understanding this trauma can empower us to live our lives with more kindness for ourselves, and ensure that we hold those responsible accountable.

To stay with the 'journey' narrative, the final stage is to truly accept who we are and to own our narrative. Many have to work extraordinarily hard to reach this point, including me. For autistic people this does not come without immense challenge. We have been taught through the ages that we are not worth anything to society, that we are second class citizens, even an embarrassment. We have been seeped in this cocktail of societal opinions until we ourselves have absorbed the bitter taste of hate. However, something is changing now. We as a collective and as individuals are learning how to accept ourselves, dare I say value ourselves. The journey narrative may be misleading, as the process I have outlined may not be linear and will be different for all autistic individuals. I know myself that I have to make the decision every day to accept and value who I am.

When we reach a point where we truly accept and value ourselves, particularly as a collective, we are taking our narratives back from the hands of those who do not understand us. We are owning our narratives and calling out narrative-theft when neurotypicals attempt to write our story themselves. This book is my effort to show that autistic people have a right to tell their own stories. When we can tell our stories, we give each other a hand to climb out of the holes we have fallen into, holes often created by a world that does not work for us. When we can own our narratives, we have the power to expose the trauma we endure at the hands of a world designed for a different kind of brain. I want the world to understand that we are here; we are here hand flapping and fidgeting; we are here not making eye contact; we are here demanding justice.

This book is for those who need to read a story and feel recognized. This book is for those who want to hear what other autistic people have found helpful when facing mental health challenges. This book is for autistic people who want to know how others have found hope. This book is for carers, professionals and others to learn and understand what autism is like and what mental health challenges we face. This book is for non-autistic people to see we are human.

Despite the difficulties and hurdles faced in pulling this together, I am immeasurably proud of myself and the contributors. I feel we have achieved my vision: to take a slice of the autism community and put it on paper. I hope you find an essay that you identify with. I hope that you can learn something about yourself, and I hope you can challenge yourself to listen to someone you may not normally hear.

Without further ado, I will let you get on and read…

# Who Am I?

MAIR ELLIOTT

## Hurt

I grew up in a white, middle-class, close-knit, typical nuclear family. To all intents and purposes, I was privileged. I was safe and loved. I lived in an innocent infant bubble. Before the age of six, I had no reason to question my place or my worth in this world. I could be who I was and pursue whatever excited me.

I recall the long summers spent at the family caravan on the Welsh coast. I would spend hours sitting mesmerized by the rock pools, catching and releasing little creatures. I allowed the experience, the learning and the pure joy to fill me up. My body felt at home among the seaweed and barnacles, with the crashing waves behind me in the distance. I could catch fish with my bare hands. I would hold them gently and study them before quickly putting them back into the water, ensuring I didn't damage their fragile bodies. My mind was fixed on these colourful miniature pools of seawater. My body, covered in salt and sand, could have melted into the landscape and I would have let it. I was at home in my head. Processing, questioning, understanding the marine life. The level of focus and attention to detail I mustered was unrivalled in those the same age as me. It eclipsed even the basic cues to eat or urinate. Rock pooling was more important. The joy I experienced on those long summer days by the sea is impossible to capture in words.

At six years old I moved school. In hindsight, this was the event which caused the first damage to my innocence. Up until then I had spent my time with my family, who accepted me unconditionally, or in pre-school with other children my age who didn't have the psychological or emotional development to question their own or anyone else's identity. However, moving into a completely new peer group created irreversible changes in how I perceived myself and my place in this world. At the time, I didn't have the ability to truly reflect on what was happening. I was only six, after all. There would be times when it felt as though nothing had changed. It seemed that I had swiftly been 'adopted' by a group of children a couple of years older than me, who provided stable friendship. Nothing had changed in my abilities in the classroom. Nonetheless, that feeling of safety I had taken for granted was slowly washing away. I started to experience moments of soul-crushing fear, and it felt as if the world was suddenly spinning faster but time was slowing down. The vulnerability that would quickly wash over me was like being thrown naked into a freezing lake. My brain changed from being very logical and linear to feeling as though someone had swapped my thoughts for an angry swarm of wasps. All I wanted was to scream, 'I DON'T UNDERSTAND.'

My mouth wouldn't move, and my face did not convey my internal struggle. It appears on reflection that, unconsciously or consciously, I knew I wasn't supposed to feel like this. I wasn't supposed to be confused by the other children's interactions. I wasn't supposed to be overwhelmed by the environment around me. I knew, somehow, that this made me vulnerable and therefore put me in danger. For whatever reason, I felt I couldn't tell anyone, not even my family, about these incidents that caused increasing damage to the foundation beneath my feet.

I knew I had to do something to protect myself. I was an analytical child; I saw an issue and I figured out the solution. The problem was me and my ever-growing inability to understand the social developments of my peers. I concluded that I was fundamentally flawed. This belief about myself, although I didn't know at the time, triggered a series of psychological and emotional events that would plague me for the remainder of my childhood and early adulthood.

I was not the kind of person to see a problem and let it go, I was going to fix it. It was here that I can say for certain that I started to mask and camouflage. The little scientist within me started to observe the behaviour, language, bodies and voices of other children. Most of this was unconscious; however, I was becoming increasingly more able to do this consciously. The more aware of this process I became, the more intelligently I could proceed. With the observations I made I could adapt my own behaviour, language, body and voice. As I started to do this, the episodes of overwhelming fear and confusion diminished. I was smart; with six- to seven-year-olds the social intricacies of my peer group weren't advanced, and neither was the schoolwork. I had the capacity to hold it all within my head. However, in hindsight, the image I get when I think about myself at this age is of me sat in my fear, building a wall around myself for protection. It felt so necessary at the time, but now I see I was slowly shutting myself off. I was building a wall around myself that, yes, would protect me, but would also trap me.

At the time all seemed well again, and I continued to develop my masking and camouflaging which allowed me to go back to feeling fairly happy and stable. I still had my family and friends.

I was good at school. I continued with my life as I should. All the while a nagging feeling of being out of place and needing to protect myself loomed in the back of my mind. It wasn't until secondary school that things started to go awry again.

Puberty is never a good time for anyone, particularly in the beginning when you don't really know what is happening. It also happens to coincide with important educational milestones. Raging hormones, social development on hyper-speed and increasing pressure from an education system that seemed more like an industrial factory for A grades than a place of safety, this was never going to end well for someone like me. With each year I attended, the dark cloud of out-of-place-ness grew. By Year 9, aged 14, the protective walls I had built around myself could rival any high-security prison. The children around me had started to explore sex, relationships and their own place in the world, turning to crude and often (in my opinion) animalistic behaviour. This turned into a pack hunt if any of them sniffed out difference. Given my ingenious solution to mask and camouflage my differences I was lucky to avoid being preyed on, most of the time. The pressure was rising, however. It felt a little as if I was in a horror movie hiding from the monster, hearing it stalk around, its breath hanging in the air, and praying it wouldn't find me.

The one thing that was on my side was my love for learning. I was smart and able to focus, particularly when it came to science and maths. Biology was my favourite; I suppose it was in my bones from birth. It almost felt that I already knew the answers, that somehow it was just intuition. Nature, animals and their inner workings was something that I had always been interested in, from the marine wildlife in rock pools to the horses I was now obsessing over at 14 years old. My connection to nature was deep enough to flow through my veins. I just loved being in most of my lessons though – the thrill of learning was everything to me. I also knew I was good; I knew I possessed a level of intelligence that most of my peers didn't have. I wouldn't dare show it off but being really smart was important to me. It felt like an extra layer of protection.

Yet, from age 14 onwards, education changes. It becomes a pressure cooker in which teachers are expected to throw kids in and get A* out. If you are in the top sets for most of your subjects, then anything below an A was unacceptable. My own perfectionism started to become destructive. I was taking 14 GCSEs and had set my mind on A* in all of them. Anything less would have been a failure in my eyes. This mindset was not helped by the constant messaging from school insinuating that if we 'failed' our exams we would fail at life. My love for school was replaced with anxiety and fear.

Between the school pressure, trying to mask and camouflage in increasingly more intricate and complex ways, and the fear I would be discovered as a failure, it doesn't surprise me that I crumbled. I feel such sadness for that little girl trying to carry the world and put a brave face on all the while. In retrospect, the darkness had been growing for a long time before I finally succumbed. In fact, it had been growing slowly and quietly ever since I was six years old. I hadn't noticed it as I was gradually shutting myself off behind my protective walls. I was scared of the outside world, when my internal world was probably what I should have been worried about. There was not some massive event to trigger anything. Nothing major happened. I didn't suddenly combust. I just decided I didn't want to eat. I was on a school trip to Stratford-on-Avon. With what I know now, I suppose, for me a school trip was a big deal, but at the time it didn't seem like something that would cause me to stop eating. I just found myself not wanting to put food in my mouth. It was as if a switch went in my brain.

People noticed of course. My friends to begin with, who then consulted with a teacher. It wasn't long before the school had told my parents. I had discovered that not eating brought about a state of numbness. I hadn't noticed how high my baseline levels of anxiety, overwhelm and fear had been until I was too numb to feel them anymore. Once I discovered I could block these feelings out by reducing the amount of food I ate, it became hard to return to a state in which I could eat 'normally' again. While I felt safer not eating, my actual situation got worse.

By the time I went into my first year of GCSEs it appeared I had hit a psychological and emotional tipping point. It was as if someone had tied boulders to my feet and chucked me into a pit. It didn't matter how well I could climb, I was not getting out. All anyone could do was try to keep me from sinking, but neither my teachers nor my parents knew how. I had started to self-harm by this point. Just like the deliberate starvation, self-harm acted as a brief escape from anxiety, fear and crushing despair. I did not really understand why I was doing these things, however. It is only in hindsight that I can understand that I was just trying to survive when I felt so close to perishing.

My complete lack of insight at the time meant I was not able to communicate these feelings to anyone effectively. Instead, it came out as a change in behaviour. I started to leave lessons halfway through, lock myself in the end cubicle of the girls' toilets for hours on end, and have sudden outbursts of either anger, panic or despair. I would just 'switch off' as if I wasn't conscious, and I wouldn't spend time with my friends or do the things I had previously enjoyed. In among all of this, I was still maintaining the masking and camouflaging. To others I would appear to be 'normal', as if nothing had changed, and then out of nowhere, for no apparent reason, I would start behaving erratically, abnormally and self-destructively. It confused everyone, including me. I had no idea what was happening to me. I couldn't form the words in my mouth to explain to anyone, I couldn't express that I was about to panic or that I was getting angry, I had no ability to form logical thoughts to define what was going on in my head. My once logical and linear brain was becoming clouded and nonsensical. Who I thought I was, was changing against my will.

I don't know if I was just lucky, or if there was something high priority about my case, but I was swiftly referred to mental health services and seen within a couple of months. Meeting a psychiatrist for the first time was weird. I couldn't mask and camouflage as well as usual because I didn't know the social protocols to follow. I was temporarily returned to a state of being socially inept and painfully exposed. I don't particularly remember the appointment, but I have since read my medical notes.

The psychiatrist outlined the following conversation:

Doctor: 'Why do we have emotions?'

Me: 'Well one assumes that at some point in the evolution of mankind an advantageous mutation occurred which gave humans emotions. Those who had this mutation survived longer and repro-duced and henceforth passed the advantageous gene to the next generation. Natural selection.'

Doctor: 'I think you are the only person to ever give me that answer...'

This little excerpt made me laugh as I read my medical notes.

This conversation I had with the psychiatrist would prove to be extraordinarily important to me and my future. At the time, I was just wondering why this quirky psychiatrist was asking me daft questions. I do not know if it was this first appointment, or if it was in a following appointment, but I distinctly remember the psychiatrist asking, 'Have you heard of autism?'

In truth, I had only the misconceptions that most of society has about autism: the kids with 'autism' were the ones in the 'special class', and they couldn't do anything useful or look after themselves. It kills me that this was my understanding of autism, and writing it here feels like a confession I should have taken to the grave. But that is the truth, and unfortunately this is how many still understand autism. When the psychiatrist asked me this question though, I didn't really have an answer for him. I think I already knew where the conversation was going. In the following sequence of events I don't ever remember rejecting the idea that I could be autistic. It felt an unusually familiar concept to me, not one that I'd ever thought about directly, yet it wasn't foreign.

Again, maybe chance or luck or there was something about my case, but I and my family underwent the autism diagnostic process swiftly. I don't really remember the details, but what I do remember is the collective process me and my family went through. My parents were, rightly, taken aback when the idea of autism was first brought up. Over time as the diagnostic tests were being done there was a sense that slowly some things were falling into place. The oh-that-makes-sense-now moments paved a way for a different understanding of my childhood. My incredible ability to focus on marine life, my insistence on lining things up as a baby, the time that I undid the laces on a shoe just to figure out how to put them back in, the infamous 'pink phase' when I would only wear pink (including pink pants and socks) – there was a reason that my 'play' didn't look like other children's play. By the time the official letter was given to us, we'd all done our own research, particularly on the role gender plays in autism, and we'd spent a considerable amount of time reflecting on and contemplating this new-found way of understanding, so the information in the letter was not surprising at all. In fact, it confirmed what had clicked in all of us.

I went to school after reading the letter. I immediately sought out the English teacher whom I had become attached to after my friends had confided in her. I had a big smile on my face. I was happy to tell her I was autistic. There was a name to those differences I had discovered nine years previously. I wasn't a failure, I was autistic. I was different, but I could have a tangible understanding as to why. Many have written about the feeling of getting a late autism diagnosis. In recent years, I have started to consider myself lucky that I was still technically a child when I got my diagnosis, as others have been halfway through their lives before finding out. It's one of the most surreal things you could go through because you are overwhelmed with relief and even joy, but you know that you live in a society that sees this as a 'sad' moment. You are also forced to go back and re-evaluate your entire existence. This process can be very painful over time however, and the way you understand yourself changes. You can start to forgive yourself for what was previously unacceptable. The oh-that-makes-sense-now moments bring wonderful little bursts of acceptance. Getting my diagnosis was life changing. I owe a lot to that psychiatrist who, by luck, had a good understanding of autism.

While this discovery was incredibly influential to understanding myself, those negative internal beliefs and the now habitual masking and camouflaging were not going to budge. The overwhelming feelings of fear and despair, the self-destructive and impulsive behaviour, the spiral downwards was not stopping for anyone or anything. As time went on, it gathered speed and power. Everyone around me could see that I was heading in a direction no-one wanted, like a speeding train heading straight down finite tracks towards a precipice. I had disappeared. As the days went by, I became more self-destructive and less able to communicate. I don't think words will ever do justice to the crushing, suffocating, unceasing pain. It buried itself down into my bones and overtook even the laws of time and space, manipulating and obscuring any sense of reality I had.

I cannot say for certain when or how, but by 16 years old I had begun to lose touch with reality and started experiencing episodes of hallucinations mixed with episodes of total dissociation, in which I couldn't remember what I'd done, where I'd been or even who I was. I had stopped being able to self-harm away from people, privately, and had no control over when or where I would hurt myself. I spent almost every night in the local emergency department. I would like to be able to write about this episode of my life, but my memory is so poor that I cannot recall most of this time. I was more frightened of myself than anything else. The only escape I could see was to die.

What is a person to do in that situation? I ask, because I still do not really know. The medical mental health system saw fit to put me in a psychiatric ward five hours away from my home. No limits or boundaries were given as to how long I'd be locked away or what would happen while I was locked away. I wrote a poem many years ago about travelling to the unit, I'd like to share it with you:

Over the horizon an orange glow
Over where the stars don't go
Fields of green flick past in seconds

Not far now the driver reckons

The world flurries, flurries past
From one village to the last
I wonder how it is my mind
Reached this state of such unwind

Sat in a car escorted by nurses
With my dad, one converses
The other keeps an eye on me
Prepared to pounce should I flee

The orange city dome approaches
As my dread and fear encroaches
Skyline replaced by staggered concrete
As I shift nervously in my car seat

Not quite sure if anything's real
Not quite sure if my mind will heal
Not quite sure where I'm headed
But this is exactly what I dreaded

My mind has gone, and in its place
Sinister, bizarre thoughts deface
I don't understand what is happening
My world is continuously blackening

Driving through the night-time city
In another mind it could be pretty
Stepping out of the car I condemn
My future to the hands of a system

Windows guarded by steel bars
From here you can't see the stars

Am I a prisoner or a patient?
We enter a guarded door adjacent

Searched and shown the psych ward
Nurse marks her suspicious clipboard
And then I realize my dad will leave
For my home and family, I grieve

One last hug before he goes
His smell lingers in his clothes
I see the door lock between us
Too devastated to show any fuss

Catching tears before they fall
I watch 'til it's just an empty hall
Between these walls I have to stay
For unknown time, 'til unknown day

I may not be a poetic genius, but I feel this poem may go some way to explain what I was going through at the time. Any child in this situation would be terrified; I think being autistic added an extra element of terror. I couldn't understand what was happening, what would happen or what had happened. My need for routine, regularity and certain comforts was brushed away without even being seen.

Reflecting on my time in that unit makes me uncomfortable. I became attached to the place, even though I saw it as a prison. It became normal to have bars on the window, to hear screaming at night, to be escorted to the 'de-escalation room' when you got distressed. It became familiar. Maybe that is why it makes me feel uncomfortable – no one, particularly a child, should ever think these things are normal. I was told I was ill and that I needed fixing. I was told that my behaviour was unacceptable, manipulative and improper. I was treated as though I was a naughty child. There were of course members of staff who didn't say these things or treat me this way, but the way in which the system spun me around left this impression.

There is a lot that I could say about the years that followed. I went through many peaks and troughs. I was in the system at varying levels. I had a number of stays in different hospitals. I nearly lost my life at some points. Lots of things happened at different levels of desirability. However, some things never changed: I still felt out of place, I still felt fundamentally flawed, and the walls that I'd built to protect myself grew higher and became ever-more imposing. I was in a constant state of survival. I learned how to play the 'game' of mental health services. I learned that the only way to be taken seriously was to be as close to death as possible. I learned how to walk the tightrope of saying enough to get some help but not saying so much that I'd get chucked into hospital. I even learned how to care for my own self-harm wounds, after too many humiliating and dehumanizing experiences in the local emergency department. Each time I got hurt by services a chunk of my ability to trust crumbled away. By the time I hit 20 years old, I had been through things that many will never experience or even understand. I had lost who I was, engulfed in a system which overshadowed every part of my being. At my core, I was just a frightened little girl who needed nothing more than safety.

## Help

When I look back, it is difficult for me to pinpoint what helped me. It isn't as simple as two binary options of 'helped' or 'didn't help'.

There are many practical things I can say that were important to my survival, such as developing the skills to do self-care (particularly when I didn't want to); having a balanced and healthy exercise routine; using sensory aids when I needed to; learning to feel comfortable stimming openly; maintaining structure and routine around sleep; learning to manage my difficulties around food; developing a healthy relationship with my body through yoga; painstakingly learning to be emotionally self-aware; addressing my perfectionism; and expressing my anger caused by my experiences of the psychiatric system. I also found out that I had a hormone problem which presented as 'mental illness', and pursuing treatment for that helped a lot.

Listing these here makes each one sound simple, yet these were things that took me a considerable amount of time and effort to engage in and develop. For a painfully long time a lot of these things felt impossible. Each one is worthy of an essay in itself, but alas I am bound by the ever-pesky word limit.

## Unmasking

A crucial part of getting well for me was to take the mask off. Over the years, the mask changed from an ingenious coping mechanism that allowed me to live, to a prison wall that I hid behind. By my late teens/early adulthood, the masking and camouflaging I was performing was incredibly intricate and complex. It had also become habitual, meaning I couldn't just stop. It was very useful in some cases; it is the reason why I am good at public speaking and I am able to sit at boards surrounded by important people and appear confident. However, the more I was masking and camouflaging, the worse my mental health became. I had to face the harsh reality that if I did not stop masking and camouflaging to the degree that I was, I would probably die at my own hands.

The major question I had to answer was: 'Who am I?'

When you have been repressing everything about yourself since you were a small child, it becomes incredibly difficult actually to know who you are. I assumed for a long time that I was the mask. That didn't sit comfortably though, and I knew deep down that there was something else to me away from the performance.

When I was finally discharged from my last stay on the acute psychiatric ward I was handed over to a psychotherapist. I obviously did not trust her, but I wouldn't have trusted anyone at that point. Yet, I wanted to try – if only for the sake of getting to a well-enough state that I could get away from the grasp services had on me.

It became obvious pretty quickly that the gap between my mask and who I actually was needed to be understood. I started by trying to recognize where, when and with whom I masked the most and least. I needed this basic information to recognize the patterns and understand why I felt I needed to mask. The next step was to take the burden of masking into account when I was planning my week. I could not understand how someone could work five days a week in an office and not get exhausted, when a single half-day would put me out of action for several days. But I had not taken into account the fact that I needed to mask and camouflage heavily in an office environment in order to be accepted socially; therefore a half-day in that workplace was incredibly exhausting. Once I knew where, when and with whom I masked the most I could start planning my week taking into account the burden of masking, ensuring that I didn't exhaust myself. Now, for example, if I have to work in an office for one day or have a day of high-level masking, I ensure that I have at least a day and a half to recoup afterwards. My recoup days are usually spent at home where I mask the least, either working on writing jobs or doing activities to bring my anxiety down.

Through doing this, I ensured I didn't push myself to burn out through masking too much. It gave me space in my head to start exploring further into my internal world. I also learned that I would never cope in an office job, and that it was unlikely I could ever work full time due to this need for recoup time. Valuable insights into my needs such as this allowed me to live with kindness for myself.

Having done the more practical things in the unmasking part of my journey, I then needed to go much deeper into exploration. This was helped along by the psychotherapist who asked very annoying and difficult questions which helped me to think about things differently. Therapy, if you do it properly, is not easy. Nevertheless, I started to trust the process a bit more, even if I couldn't fully trust the therapist due to my past experiences. I started by looking back at who I was before I started masking heavily. At the little girl whose special interest was the sea and its creatures. The little girl who refused to take her red fluffy hat off, even to go to sleep; the little girl who was smart and funny. She was a little tomboy, but I had spent years trying to fit in by wearing tons of makeup and wearing the clothes other girls wore. She loved being in the sea, but I had stopped because I thought others would judge me. She would take her teddy bear everywhere, but I stopped because 'grown-ups can't have teddies with them'. She was happy, I was not. I started to notice the crevasse between who she was and who I thought I had become.

It didn't seem like rocket science to me; I needed to retrace my steps and go back to the point that I was last happy. I don't mean by physically going back to being and behaving like a little girl but trying to do things like that little girl did. I started by reducing and finally stopping wearing makeup. The more I thought about it, the more I realized that I actually hated wearing makeup. It meant having to wake up earlier to put it on. When it was on it was itchy and set off my sensory sensitivity. I could never get it perfect, so it would irk me all day long. It made my skin unhealthy and acne covered. However, I felt safer wearing it. It was almost like a physical mask to match my social mask. I started to wear makeup to try and fit in with my peers at school; this then morphed into wearing it because society implied that women needed to wear makeup to count as feminine. Once I realized I couldn't give a sh*t whether society saw me as feminine or not, it became easier to stop wearing makeup. I was a tomboy before anyway.

Please don't get me wrong, I am not saying wearing makeup is bad. If someone enjoys wearing makeup, then that's great. For me, though, I was wearing makeup for all the wrong reasons and it made me miserable. Despite it being difficult to stop at the time, it also felt incredibly freeing. Bizarrely, I feel more confident now without makeup. It was also an important step in my journey to take the mask off. It was almost as if taking the physical mask of makeup off allowed me to keep taking steps towards fully removing the social mask. It was the taste test for unmasking.

Over a process of exploration into myself I started to realize that I would frequently put others' needs above my own, irrespective of how uncomfortable I was. I would destroy myself just to ensure others were comfortable. Masking and camouflaging were a big part of that. I felt that by being myself and not masking, I would make others uncomfortable somehow. I don't quite understand why; it was a belief that was developed early on and had never been questioned. From this fundamental belief, a weird saviour complex had developed in me by which I had to sacrifice my own health and well-being to help others. Looking back, I reckon this came into full fruition when I started my activism work. I think I needed to feel as if I mattered, that I was being 'useful'. Sacrificing myself was a way of showing how useful I could be.

In the end, it came down to a simple decision: carry on valuing others above myself or learn to value my own happiness and well-being above other people's comfort. I had tried the first option from a young age, and it did not work. I therefore spent a long time (still spend a long time) teaching myself to value my own happiness and health. That means saying 'no' to people, establishing, maintaining and communicating my boundaries, and learning to ignore the fear of being judged. I make it sound easy, but it wasn't (still isn't). I don't like saying 'no' to people and I don't like feeling as though I'm letting people down. However, unless I actively work towards valuing myself as a human being, then I will never be truly happy. In order not only to survive, but to thrive, I must see myself as I see others: important, valued and deserving of peace.

This leads me to my last point in my unmasking journey: letting myself feel joy again. Somewhere along the way while my mask grew, I had lost the ability to give myself permission to feel joy. I have a strong suspicion that the health services reinforced the idea that I was not allowed to feel joy, because as soon as I expressed joy, I would get dangerously close to losing what little support I had.

Autistic joy is a wonder to behold, but outsiders may not see it that way. While I find witnessing other autistic people's joy infectious and heart-warming, others may see the hand flapping and 'squee' noises as weird and uncomfortable. For a long time, I suppressed my autistic joy and then as a consequence I just stopped feeling joy. I feared being judged. I didn't want to lose the social standing I had managed to scrape together by hand flapping and expressing joy in an autistic way. Not knowing I was autistic for most of my childhood didn't help with these feelings. As I started to work on valuing myself, I noticed this suppression of joy I was doing and had been doing unconsciously since childhood. I actually found it really frightening to give myself permission to feel joy. I pushed forward attempting to let go of old conditioning and bring forth the joy. I wasn't really getting anywhere until I re-discovered the sea.

You may recall that I explained my feelings about the sea and its creatures at the beginning. At the age of 20, I finally gave myself permission to go back to the sea. I had, of course, been going to the beach throughout the years but I never really allowed myself to go as I had gone when I was little – with the passion, dedication and playfulness I had in heaps as a little girl. Where had that playfulness gone? Where was my dedication and passion for the sea? The answer: it was there the entire time, I just didn't let myself feel it. At 20 years old, I put my swimming costume back on and let my body melt into the ocean water again. I let myself be playful and silly, splashing and jumping through the waves. I let myself fall back in love with the water. Joy burst through me, as though it had awakened from a long hibernation. It felt like going home.

Being in water, particularly the ocean, consumes and soothes my senses. The way the water holds my weight and flows playfully through my fingers gives me something that no other place, person or thing can give me. The moment I let my body melt into the water, I can feel my internal world softening and releasing any pain (emotional or otherwise). My energy is renewed and I am free, liberated from the unrelenting stresses of being autistic in a neurotypical world. At the time of writing, the water has been unusually calm, and I have been in the sea every day. I get up in the early morning and go before anyone else emerges from their homes. It is approaching the pup season for the seals; a juvenile seal has been hanging around off the beach I frequent, waiting for its comrades to also return. I wade into the water to allow myself to float peacefully, admiring the stillness. Each morning the seal pops its head up, curiously looking at me. We acknowledge each other's presence, accepting the space the other needs. It feels like a lifetime, but seconds later we draw the wordless communication to a close and continue going about our business independently. I am more deeply connected to that seal than I can ever be with the vast majority of humankind. The wordless conversation we have contains more emotion and meaning than I would ever be able to express vocally to another human. This connection is my joy.

I am an advocate for joy. I have come to believe that success (as defined by the rich, white, cisgender, able-bodied, neurotypical, straight men who hold most of the power in industrialized countries) may bring you a sense of achievement, but joy at its raw and fundamental level is why we thrive. To have the confidence to be so vulnerable that you can experience joy is my idea of magic. Vulnerability is a key part of joy; to experience joy is to allow yourself to be open, to show honestly who you are and what you are about. It is a great and dangerous thing to give yourself permission to feel joy.

## Defining my experiences and who I am

In the past few months, while having to consider writing my story for you here, I have been looking at how I define my experience. For a very long time I was a disciple of the medical model. I believed in the language of illness and the teachings of the *Diagnostic and Statistical Manual (DSM)*.[34] I almost craved diagnoses; they gave my experiences meaning. I was led to believe that this was *the* way, the only way. I surrendered my agency to the almighty doctor who would work their cure magic and make me worthy of a normal life again. I was a good girl (at the beginning anyway), I took their pills and listened to their preachings from their swivel-chair pulpits. I had faith in the notion that sick people were defective and needed to be fixed by those who earned their power through devotion.

You may find my analogy with religion uncomfortable, but I want you to feel uncomfortable. Why? Because healthcare is not a religious institution. Please don't misunderstand me, religion is not wrong. I am not criticizing religion; I am, however, seriously questioning the damage done by having a healthcare system that revolves around a single language, a single theory, a single way of understanding pain.

I don't ever recall voluntarily surrendering all my power to a doctor with a god complex. I asked for help. I asked for support. I asked to be listened to. I asked to have my pain understood. I never asked to be persecuted. When and why was I swept up and converted into this institution where I had no power, agency or credibility? How did I become so deeply entrenched in this way of thinking that I believed it all?

I don't know what made me draw back and question the validity or usefulness of this way of framing my difficulties. Was it the long list of diagnoses, which kept growing each time a new doctor looked at my file? Or maybe it was the fact that I had so many files about me that they were held together with a bungee cord, but I had no idea what was in those files? Was it the lengthy stays in hospital that seemingly made me worse? Was it the potent drugs that made me feel so physically unwell that it wasn't worth the mild improvement in my 'behaviour'? Or perhaps it was the demeaning, dehumanizing, patronizing, gaslighting, coercing attitude of the system?

You may notice that I have rarely used medical language when explaining my story. This is intentional. I lived as an undiagnosed autistic person, unaware that my different way of perceiving and understanding the world and myself was neurological. I grew up thinking that I was fundamentally flawed. I grew up in a world that not only did not accept difference but actively damaged those who were different. I was a child forced to learn that she did not belong, that she was wrong in all senses of the word. She grew up having to break herself down, to rebuild a defensive wall for protection. This was an unreasonable expectation of a child who just wanted to feel safe. I look back now, at the edge of a new era in my life, and realize my pain was not illness. My pain was a reasonable response to an unreasonable situation.

What made me ill was the act of diagnosing me with illness. As soon as that happened, I became trapped into a single way of understanding and expressing my pain. I could no longer describe how I felt, I could only give symptoms. Dead-end, meaningless symptoms. I became so entrenched in the medical model that it penetrated down to my core. My very personality was up for poking and prodding with the pages of the diagnostic manual. I could no longer assign myself with genuine personality traits, I saw myself as a scrambled mixture of symptoms and diagnoses.

It was only when I really started to force myself into a process of self-exploration that I started to scrutinize the lens I was given to see my pain through. Backed up by my study of yoga philosophy and more recently Intentional Peer Support,[35] both offering alternative languages for understanding pain, I widened my point of view going forward. I also had new languages to enable me to go back and reflect on my experiences.

I realize that the illness language and the institution around that language forced me down a path of learned helplessness and victimhood. I was destined to be in the role of 'helpee' for what could have been my entire life. In a way, it was incredibly narcissistic. I don't like thinking about myself in those terms, but the reality is that I was put into a position that was all about me, a singular. It was not, and is not, a two-way street when it came to mental health care. Perhaps I even started to believe that I needed fixing by somebody else because of this.

When I asked for help, I sought connection. I sought understanding and empathy from a fellow human being. I was met with disconnection and humiliation from a faceless and powerful system. In fact, at my darkest times, it was not only a social disconnection but a physical one too. At my darkest times, it was not only humiliation but a violation of my space and my body. I can't help but feel outrage when I take my experience away from medical language and put it into emotive language. My feelings were stripped of meaning because I was 'sick'. My way of communicating pain was demonized. My existence was boiled down to the words written in my medical notes.

The most infuriating part for my empathetic side is that I am a white, middle-class, cisgender person with a stable and supportive family; I am privileged in multiple ways. If my experience of the system was bad, then how will others in less privileged positions fare? While I go on the lifelong unlearning of the various 'isms' I have unconsciously picked up, I do not know how to help those currently in the system.

As you may tell from the edge to my words, I am still very angry. While my experiences of the system still provide plenty of kindling for my anger, having multiple new ways of understanding my past and my present gives me an ability to see a future. How

I define my experiences may not appear to be significant on the surface, yet it has importance down to the constitutional level. How I define myself and my experiences affects how I feel about myself, how I interact with the world and, to a certain extent, how others interact with me. Taking back my story from the medical model and allowing myself to define my experiences as I want and choose to define them gave me back my agency, my power and my boundaries. I could start to see myself as a human being again and not a list of symptoms. I could rebuild a meaningful connection to myself and the world I inhabit. I could be me for the first time in a very long time.

You may be asking what the difference between autism and mental illness is, and why I am happy saying I am autistic but unhappy saying I'm mentally ill. Autism to me is not a defect or a problem. By saying 'I am autistic', it simply describes my neurotype. Of course, I have my difficulties, but the majority of these difficulties are caused by an inflexible society that refuses to accept and accommodate difference. All in all, autism, in itself, is not pain to me. 'Mental illness' is a single theory and construct to understand psychological pain. This theory does not work for me, so I changed which theory I apply to myself.

You may also be wondering whether I believe mental illness exists? I believe mental illness exists for those who find it helpful to define their experience using medical language. The medical model is not wrong, it is not an invalid way of describing pain. Medication, diagnoses and symptoms are important to many people – and that is okay. The problem arises when it is the only model or theory used to care for and support people in distress, particularly when that one theory requires a significant power imbalance.

I choose to define myself as an autistic person. I choose to define my experiences as significant distress due to the trauma of growing up unaware of my neurotype. This distress became so overwhelming it made me do things, believe things and see things that were often unconsciously intended to be self-destructive. My distress was interpreted by a system using the medical model of care, which caused even more damage in the long run. Many of the people I met in services over the years were exceedingly kind and did their best to help me, but the system would often override their good intentions. I also define myself as a strong-willed and stubborn person who loves nature, particularly the ocean. I am weird and I love it. I prefer the company of animals, but I also have a deep empathy for my fellow human beings. I work very hard to stay true to my values of honesty, integrity and kindness. I embrace joy and silliness wherever and whenever I can. All the while I am a person who likes to think deeply and inquisitively about the nature of myself, the world around me and life.

## Hope

When I proposed this structure of hurt, help and hope to the publishers, I thought 'hope' would be the easiest part of the essay for me. As it turns out, I am struggling to create a coherent set of paragraphs. I have had an inconsistent relationship with hope. For a long time, I never allowed myself to feel hope. After all, in the pit of despair there isn't any room for something so bright. After a while, I found I was becoming terrified of being hopeful. If I had too much hope, then it would hurt all the more when I crashed back down to reality. I think I confused blind optimism with hope for a while. I thought hope was foolish, and if it wasn't evidenced then it was dangerous. I look back now and see that I was, first, in distress and had no ability to critically appraise my situation so I was always going to see the negative and never the positive, and second, I was in a system that revolved around the 'bad stuff', which only made my inability to see the positive worse.

It is hard to feel hopeful when you live in a society that doesn't accept you and, in some cases, wishes you dead. I am also deeply sensitive to the world around me, and I find it incredibly hard to feel hopeful when I see the socio-economic climate, political game-playing, the climate emergency (that those in power don't seem to be doing anything about), the loss of biodiversity, genocides, wars and so on. Human beings scare me and infuriate me.

With all of that in mind though, I think I have always held hope within me somewhere. I couldn't show it, as that would have been a sign that I wasn't deserving of support from the medical mental health system. I also couldn't let myself believe in it, even though it was there. The elephant in the room, you could say. I know it was there because I reckon I would have died if it wasn't. I just never looked it in the eye.

I am not religious, but I do believe in the importance of faith and spirituality. Faith doesn't have to be in a deity or god, it can be in anything. I feel that hope is a type of faith. It's faith that the progression of time will bring change. I think after everything I have been through, everything that I have survived, I have far more capacity to have faith. To trust that things will change with time. I do think that to hope is a skill that one can embrace or reject. I must actively choose to hope and trust that I won't get hurt. If I did not do this, I would still be in that pit of despair.

There are some things about humans that give me hope, for example the autism community. In recent years, the community has grown and has become ever more confident to fight for our right to own our narratives and to have a say in matters affecting us as autistic people. The community can be fractious due to the black and white nature of our thinking, so sometimes I take a step back. However, there are always autistic peers who will listen and empathize when one of us is having a rough time. I draw hope from my peers in other communities, particularly the world of Intentional Peer Support.[35] I see a future when I see my colleagues, friends and peers fighting for social change.

Over the past year, in my journey of self-exploration, I have found many answers about myself, one of which is that I have an innate ability to find hope, as long as I give that part of me room to breathe. Masking and camouflaging suffocated that part of me. Often the world of humans suffocates that part of me. If I go into self-destruct, then that part of me suffocates. The major resource I draw from, to give that part of me breathing space, is nature. When I get up and go for a swim in the sea in the early morning; when I have the beach and the sea to myself; when the air is still and the only sound is the gentle rolling of the waves, and a gannet flies along next to me on its eternal search for fish, I feel as if I am home. I feel that I am returning to a place I should never have left. That is where I feel the peace that I have been searching for. I often think that I must be a descendant of a selkie, a part-seal, part-human creature from Celtic folklore.

There is certainty in the way nature marches on. Seeds will always germinate, flowers will always bloom, birds will continue to fly. Connection to this infinite cycle gives me a profound sense of hope. I don't know how to explain how rooted to my very survival this connection to nature is. If I could, I would grow gills, swim away and never return to the human world again. In reality, the best I could do is to go off-grid and live as a social outcast in the wild. In fact, there was an old lighthouse for sale off the coast where I live. It is built on a rock that sticks out of the ocean. It is my dream to buy that lighthouse and live there – I think I would be endlessly happy out there with the company of the dolphins and fish. For now, at least, I must continue to live as a part of society.

Hope is such an abstract thing. It is different for all of us. I do think that the demands of our modern life suffocate our innate ability to hope. I have found that the less I engage with social media, consumer culture and the endless catastrophizing news out there, the happier I feel. Perhaps that is just me though; I have always been incredibly happy with my own company away from the industrial drone of modern humans.

Do I have hope for myself? Yes. I trust in the process of change and the passing of time. I am given hope by my deep and nurturing connection to nature. I have hope for myself and my future. I realize now that hope is a key component of thriving, and so I invest in the factors that pave a way to being hopeful. I have found a way to be at peace – and that is a magical and hope-inspiring thing.

I am now in a place in my life in which I am vividly happy, with a profound sense of internal contentment. I am glad I am alive; I am grateful I can live my life as myself. Even on the inevitable rough days when the world seems to be against me as an autistic person, I have a kindness for myself.

I think that many autistic people, including my past self, believe that we will never be able to be truly happy, that the trauma we experience as individuals and as a collective will always hinder our path to happiness. My trauma hasn't gone, it is now a part of who I am; however, it did not stop me from finding health and happiness. It didn't come served on a plate though, I worked extraordinarily hard to get to where I am now. In fact, I still work incredibly hard every day. That's not to say that society and its systems shouldn't be held accountable, of course they should. My point is that happiness is not an unachievable goal. It is an act of defiance to find a way to be truly happy in a world that could, and tries to, burn us down. My happiness is my war cry.

There is a word in Welsh (my language): 'hiraeth'. It does not translate very easily, but it roughly means a deep and heart-aching longing for a place or a thing that was/is 'home'. When I say 'home' I mean it in its most spiritual and profound way. I truly think that for all those years I suffered, it was 'hiraeth', a longing for my most profound and spiritual home. I found it in myself, and I found it in the sea.

# I Don't Really Wanna Fight No More

MORÉNIKE GIWA ONAIWU

## Hurt

Once upon a time there was a teenage girl.

She met a boy her age, and they connected. And on and off for the next decade and a half, more on than off, they were together. She loved him. He loved her. But the relationship, once sweet and loving, eventually became hurtful and sick.

Some of the toxicity might have been due to youthful ignorance and the typical problems that plague young relationships. However, a sizable portion of it was likely due to the fact that they were initially connected not by common interests or mutual friends, but by a 'trauma bond', which later led to co-dependence and abuse.

There were certainly an unlikely couple. They lived on different sides of town. Their religious backgrounds were different. She was an honours student; he didn't care much for school. Her skin was the colour of coffee; his was the colour of cream. She liked science fiction; he preferred video games. Her ebony hair was big and puffy like cotton candy, while his hair was sleek and straight. She grew up eating her family's West African cuisine such as pounded yam and egusi; his family was American, and he grew up eating pot roast and pasta. Their neurology was different too – although not yet formally diagnosed, she was on the autism spectrum; he was not.

Yet in some very significant ways they had a great deal of similarities. They had both survived childhood abuse; they had both endured loss; they had both constructed a protective internal shell to shut out potential predators, but, unfortunately, it also kept out potential supporters. Additionally, both shared the experience of 'not belonging' in the world they occupied, and struggling with a sense of being rejected for being 'different'. Within one another they found acceptance and support, and from that a strong emotional bond (formed from shared histories of trauma) developed, followed by a relationship that spanned over half of their lives.

Over time, the boundaries of what had once been their distinct identities began to blur, and they bled into one another. Fused by love, but also by co-dependence, they both lost who they used to be and became something new. Something that was occasionally beautiful, but because they were both broken, it also became ugly – jealous, insecure, incomplete and unhealthy.

Seeds of dissension began to take root and it became apparent that both the ease with which they once interacted and the openness and trust they shared were only surface level. Resentment, bitterness and suspicion festered within them – particularly in him, but also in her. Their relationship began to resemble a battlefield, and they were both ruthless warriors; kindness, respect, trust and compassion were the first casualties. Self-worth, integrity and fidelity were soon to follow. Their lives became a blur: days filled with quarrels; nights filled with make-up sex; and their hearts and minds both compromised.

Years passed. She sometimes wondered when she looked at him, his face red and contorted with rage during yet another argument, his fists balled and voice raised, what had happened to her best friend, her soulmate. And whether she cowered from his blows in fear, as she did some days, or became infuriated and screamed at him, as she did other days, she wondered what had happened to her too. Where had their love got poisoned? Why couldn't they get past this period? When would the unhappiness go away? And how, with everything collapsing on them, could she still feel such a deep, consuming love for him, even when he filled her with disgust or anger or fear?

Things got bad and then they got worse. Yet she still loved him. She broke every rule, every standard she had ever had, for him. She tolerated things she had promised herself she would never accept from any man. She began to hate who she had become, but not enough to be without him. Her love for him, the only love she had ever felt for any man, had grown so large, so powerful, so consuming that it nearly asphyxiated her. And though her self-esteem was shredded and her psyche trampled, he still set her heart soaring and her body ablaze. Despite the tears, the fighting, the pain, the lies, the disrespect, and even the fear, living without him was not an option. Any hurt their union caused paled in comparison to the pain of being apart from him. When they feuded and separated, she could feel physical pain – sharp, stabbing agony in her abdominal region – from his absence. She was co-dependent, she was addicted, she no longer knew who she was without him. She needed his presence, his love, his embrace, his reassurance, his touch to feel alive. She was no longer anyone if she was not part of him. She belonged to him, and he to her, and that was the most real thing they both knew.

He could make her feel so high and at the same time so low. She sustained herself on the good moments. The hours they would spend engrossed in conversation as they lay in bed at night. The inside jokes they shared, and how they could laugh so long and hard with one another that hysterical tears came. The invigorating debates they had about various philosophical concepts. Sentimental moments together on anniversaries, birthdays and holidays. Nights of passion that still took her breath away and infused her body with ecstasy and fulfilment. Whispered promises to one another, and plans, and dreams, and potential. The good times were so good. She could see the love in his eyes when he gazed at her, could feel the light from his smile. When things were good with them, all was right with the world.

But bad moments were frequent, and when it was bad, it was really bad. Cornering her in the closet where no one could hear her muffled screams as he pummelled her mercilessly when he was in a rage. Strings of lies and inconsistencies, and gaslighting when she dared to refute his false narratives. Recurring infidelity (though he denied cheating, both the baby he conceived with another woman and the sexually transmitted infection he gave her demonstrated otherwise). Disappearing money when bills and rent were due. Unusually high mileage on their vehicle. Paranoia, irritability and erratic mood swings. Irrational outbursts that were no longer contained within their home and now occurred in front of his family, their friends and even at her job. Constant accusations; manipulation and argument-baiting; threats and games and more lies. Countless broken promises.

The abuse continued and her despair grew. He treated her like crap and treated himself worse. She had never been hurt so badly by another human being in her life, especially one who professed to love her. Despite how badly he treated her, she still loved him. And because she knew how sick that was, she hated herself for it, for still loving him even as his 'love' was destroying them both. She left him. She came back. She left again. She came back. He left. He came back. Resentful, she secretly found someone else to be with – a revenge affair that blossomed out of control before she could cut it off, before she could keep from getting caught. He left. He came back. She left again. But she came back. She couldn't stay away. She always came back.

She couldn't leave, not really. She couldn't quell the insatiable yearning for him – to hear his voice, to feel his breathing against hers as he slept, to kiss him on his eyes, to hear him tell her he was sorry and it wouldn't happen again and he was going to change and please believe in him and he could never love anyone else the way he loved her and that he only hurt her because he was scared to lose her and didn't mean it. He told her he would kill himself if things ended between them, and she believed it, as she had been driven to try to take her own life more than once during low periods.

She knew they were hurting and dragging one another down, but neither could or would end things. He lost himself in marijuana, in alcohol, in opiates, in other women, in furtive porn usage. She lost herself in anger, in long hours at work, in increasing anxiety and debilitating depression, in food, in self-harm (scratching herself until she bled on her upper arms and other areas easily hidden by clothing; pulling her hair out at the roots to the point where she needed hairpieces to hide the bald parts of her scalp).

It didn't make any sense – except it did, because nothing about their relationship made sense to anyone, even to them. It was like a dream at times and like a nightmare at times. It felt as if neither of them would ever rouse from their gilded cage; that they would continue to drift along, breaking away pieces of themselves until there was nothing left, and still refusing to let go.

## Help

The day that she left for good started out like any other. She went to work; he left their home to go do God knows what, as usual (she'd learned by this point not to question his whereabouts, but supposedly he was out 'job-hunting'). Though she didn't start the day with any concrete plans to end things, within a few hours her world was torpedoed by the accidental discovery of yet another betrayal. In some ways, this latest news was not as bad as many of the other indiscretions that preceded it, though cumulatively she had endured so much it was becoming hard to gauge anymore. However, the raw pain and indignation of the most recent circumstances temporarily awakened something within her, and in that moment of clarity and momentary courage, before she lost her nerve, she took the remainder of the day off work and called some friends to come over quickly and help her move her things out before he returned.

She cried alone in her bed night after night as she began the process of withdrawing from him, of extracting what was left of who she had been and trying to heal. The leaving itself was not the hardest part; she had left him before. Her biggest struggle was not going back. She didn't know if she was going to be able to follow through as she never had before. She didn't know if she was going to be able to stay away from him – and in fact, at times she faltered and momentarily resumed contact with him. But gradually she gained a bit of strength and was able to resist, to talk herself out of it, to point out to herself the inconsistencies in his words and actions. To be less afraid. To start the process of re-establishing a little bit of her dignity.

She realized that breaking free of this was not something she could do alone, and she reached out for help. Psychiatric care was a helpful resource for her in terms of navigating the emotional triggers, depression and anxiety she faced. Despite a nearly lifelong aversion to any notion that she 'needed' medication, she convinced herself to take her meds as prescribed to give them a chance to work. She got herself into weekly therapy after carefully vetting some therapists to find one who seemed like a good fit. By using the Employee Assistance Program (EAP) offered by her employer, her first three sessions were free, and her insurance benefits picked up the remaining costs apart from a minimal co-pay that she was responsible for.

Though she had hidden most of the abuse from her parents, she began to confide regularly in a few of her friends as well as her siblings, seeking encouragement to help her garner the strength not to answer his calls, not to go see him, not to reach out to him. She started visiting a church regularly and eventually confided in a few people that she had befriended there about what she was going through. Those people assured her that they would pray regularly about her situation, which she appreciated greatly.

She also lurked on online message boards and groups that specifically addressed intimate partner violence. She did not feel comfortable posting yet, but reading about others who had been in her predicament and survived made her feel less alone. She began to record her thoughts and feelings, especially on the hard days. She wrote several letters to him 'getting her feelings out' and then ripped them up so she would not be tempted to send them. Gradually, she began to feel more confident that maybe, just maybe, this time she would be able to do it, that she was stronger than she believed herself to be.

It took multiple months and more than a few failed attempts to finally sever all ties and disentangle herself from him. Frustratingly, even when she succeeded at maintaining no contact, she found that she still couldn't entirely erase him from her mind. He still had power over her, only now it had changed. What had once been love evolved into fury at how she had been mistreated, and disappointment in herself for her role in allowing it to happen.

Rather than longing for him and craving his presence, now anger kept her up at night seething with rage about everything she'd been through. When she was finally able to fall asleep, she dreamt night after night about getting revenge, usually in a violent manner, often waking up drenched in sweat. This continued until she realized that being consumed by anger meant that she was still in bondage, just in a different way, because she still thought about him constantly, but with hatred instead of love. She realized that she needed to move on; she needed to let him go.

But how?

She could not just 'forgive and forget' and go off into the sunset! Not after all of that pain; not after she had wasted nearly half her life. He *didn't* deserve her forgiveness, and she knew she would *never* forget what had happened.

How could she ever be released from this? How could she get past it? She realized that if she didn't find a solution, she would forever remain his victim. And that was unacceptable; she had been victimized long enough. She decided that even though she was tired of fighting, she still needed to fight. For her sanity. For her future. For herself.

It was hard work, but she persevered. For the first time in her life, she adhered faithfully to her medication regime and maintained her therapy appointments. At her therapist's request, she increased the frequency of her sessions. Gradually, she embarked on the difficult task of addressing some of her early life trauma. She had never truly faced it and knew that it had contributed to her susceptibility to manipulation and abuse. She also worked on forgiving herself for being an enabler who'd allowed others to mistreat her. She made efforts to affirm herself and began to establish healthy boundaries to protect herself. In time, she was able to internalize that even though she was responsible for making poor choices, she was not responsible for the abuse; it was *not* her fault. She deserved better.

She began to practise self-care and to try to process her own feelings – something she had never really prioritized before. In the process, she leaned into aspects of her autistic identity to help herself self-regulate, particularly self-stimulatory behaviours, repetitive patterns and perseverative thinking. She made a playlist of carefully selected songs and would listen to them over and over again. Shortly afterwards, she did the same thing, but with a video playlist of different clips from movies and shows that had special meaning for her.

She read certain books and certain parts of books over and over again. Other times, she purchased and ate specific foods for comfort. She chose a particular time of day after work to go on daily walks, taking the same predetermined route for continuity. She hung a calendar on her wall and began to mark each day that she successfully resisted the urge to self-harm, and would often glance at the growing number of consecutive marks for encouragement.

She was not sure exactly when it happened as it happened subtly, in what sometimes felt like microscopic increments as she worked on herself. But in time, she shed much of the guilt that she had harboured for years, and in doing so, she gained herself.

## Hope

That young lady was, and is, me. At times, all of this feels so removed from the life that I have now that it's hard to reconcile that it was my reality. But it was.

For a very long time, after I had obtained a sense of closure and healing, I felt that it was in my best interest not to revisit these events. I think that was a healthy choice for me to make at that time. However, a few years ago, things changed.

Gradually, I started to identify as an abuse survivor. At first, just a little here and there; over time, a little more and a little more. It was quite difficult to do at first, and frankly, in some ways it still is. For even though I am in some ways a pretty open person, this isn't an easy topic to discuss. It leaves me feeling very naked, very vulnerable. And because I had pushed it out of my mind for so long and it isn't part of my present, in some ways it would probably be easier to just leave it where I placed it and never bring it up again.

However, 'easier' isn't necessarily 'better'. Society in general is often silent about the connection between imbalanced power dynamics in relationships and abuse. This is exponentially problematic for autistic people because our interdependence on family, friends, significant others and other caregivers tends to be more easily recognizable to observers than that of non-autistic individuals. There is nothing wrong with needing support, but unfortunately it can result in power dynamics that put us at risk and help to fuel a culture of secrecy, shame, gaslighting and continued abuse. I no longer live a life plagued with emotional and physical abuse, but I once did, and I hope that what I have been through and what I have learned can help someone else.

So many autistic people think something like this will never happen to them. Others who have unfortunately experienced some form of abuse before might rationalize their current circumstances or console themselves with the adage that 'it could be worse'. Conversely, some of us might not perceive what is happening as abuse because we are accustomed to being made to feel that we are deficient, 'hard to deal with', oversensitive or incapable of good decision making.

Others might stay out of a sense of loyalty to the abuser(s). Additionally, many of us who are on the spectrum rely on the abuser(s) financially, medically, emotionally or otherwise, and therefore feel trapped in their situation. And often, if we do try to access support to leave the abuser(s), we find that many of the external resources that exist are extremely inaccessible for us and therefore we might determine that remaining with the abuser(s) seems to be the 'lesser of two evils'. There are infinite scenarios as well as infinite reasons why an individual might experience abuse. Regardless of the differences, one thing remains true in every circumstance: nothing we have done justifies what is being done to us.

Abuse changes you. You're never the same. But although it might have scarred me, it didn't beat me. It didn't destroy me. I am still here, and I am free.

Disclosure is a very individualized matter, and though I have opted to share my story, the choice to remain private is also a completely valid one that should be respected. My purpose for sharing my experiences is to generate hope.

I want better for us, and I have hope that a better future – one with healthy, fulfilling, reciprocal and loving relationships devoid of abuse – is possible.

I want to share a message of truth, hope and encouragement with my community in particular, the autistic people who are reading this. And especially any of you who suspect that you might be experiencing abuse, please heed my words carefully.

Dear one, I come to you as a kinsperson and friend, casting no blame on you nor shame. I have been where you are. I have. I dwelled there for much of my life – in that place of limbo induced by love and quiet hope. I know what you're hoping for, and I know why. I know how much of yourself you've invested and that you can envision a future so much better than this one because your relationship has so much potential. I know you sometimes, maybe many times, think you can fix this. Maybe you've even glimpsed what you hope to be progress.

I know how deeply you love. That love can, to you, feel as if it is absolutely, positively, 100 per cent authentic. The reality of your circumstances doesn't negate the feelings that you possess. Perhaps sometimes you are disgusted with yourself (like I was) because that love persists. Please don't be. You aren't foolish, and you aren't weak; you are human. You're not a bad person because you love someone/something that causes you pain. But it *does* mean that this love is unhealthy for you. It *does* make it bad for you – harmful for you.

My friend, 'love' is not enough. You need more than just love to survive. If that which you love continuously crushes you, constantly causing you immense pain, then that love is not for you – and truthfully, it is not real love. Though real love might – no, will – sometimes have painful moments because like anything else that matters, it requires work, it should not eat away at your soul. That's not love – at least not a healthy love.

You are worth so, so, so much more than that faded caricature that is masquerading itself as true love. Let it go. Be open to the real, lasting love that is meant for you. You have to discard the love that maims to make room for the love that fulfils. The love that will not destroy you from within but will instead fit seamlessly into your heart and into your messy life; the love that will complement who you already are as well as who you will come to be.

It will be a love that will cause you to grow in a way that only reassuring, stable and healthy love can do; it will be a love that will cause you to glow in a way that only reassuring, stable and healthy love can do. This is love that heals, not hurts; builds up, not tears down; loves instead of lies. It is real, and it is the love you – and I – always deserved.

Choose you, and wait, my friend. That love is coming. Maybe it is the love you will come to develop within yourself – a deep sense of love and regard for yourself. Maybe it is love from someone else – a future partner who will cherish you. Maybe it's a spiritual love. Maybe it's a combination. But whatever it is, it is coming. And it is real and it is beautiful – just like you.

# Hurting, Helping and Hoping

## From Learning to Diagnosis and Contentment

PAUL STATHAM

I grew up alongside the foothills of the English Cotswolds escarpment, with pleasurable walks after school, and week-long cycle rides, courtesy of a long-missed friend and the reliable but necessarily cheap Youth Hostels Association. Cosy parents in a warm home supported my basic needs. In those distant far-off times, another era, another country, mental health was never talked about, and autism was not knowable, save for unfortunate souls incarcerated in lifelong institutions that were only ever mentioned in whispered, hushed, embarrassed tones.

I knew I was different, but I did not know what the variance was. I had no reference points, no social media barometer. I had no words, and no means of expression. I was poor at sports, thanks to still dreadfully inadequate fine motor skills and off-target hand-eye co-ordination. I was socially but happily outcast, immersing myself inside academic achievements, books, railways and the ever-verdantly remembered countryside.

# Hurting

## Hurting the first time

That feeling of feeling different did not cause pain, just curiosity and wonder. I sat alone on the bus heading towards school. Even when my school coat was sodden by bullies in the showers after rugby I did not feel pain. Even when I was chased by a rival school's hard gang after I had alighted the bus, it did not cause pain, but...

They wanted me to do things early. Get the mathematics and the English out of the way they said to me. Pass the O-levels at 14 instead of 16 they said, it will leave you more time to focus on other topics in two years' time.

A coterie of us so-called gifted pupils began cramming, that strange feeling of doing more than you should, which still haunts me today. Trying to shove in more tasks to fit inside artificially less time started those panicky but real and tangible sensations of heart palpitations and nausea. I started getting stomach cramps and dreading school. The feeling of things crashing out of control. Of wanting and striving for perfection, but knowing I was set up for defeat. The giddiness and light-headedness and sleepless nights contributing to a concentration span evaporating like a puddle made from spring rain, followed by a burst of sunshine. The buttery, slippery sensations of things, time, topics and knowledge passing through your fingers, but you are unable to grasp or hold on to anything.

I had not heard of anxiety in those days. I could not articulate the sensations but they were ever present.

My mother became worried and looked at me with a knotted brow, perplexed at how her son was not coping when he had excelled previously. My dad, keen for me to progress, but not understanding, left me isolated. I could not speak to my friend about it as he was not in our so-called elite little group, and we had no shared experience to which we could relate.

Miraculously, I passed. Not with flying colours, not with a fanfare, not with A grades, but the Bs were not to be belittled. It was done with, and was out of the way.

## On track again

The next two years were a blur of study, practice and more mock examinations. I had not given any thought as to what would happen when it was all over. Did school end? School was my life, so how could it? I had not articulated to myself what I was studying for, or for whom.

We were to attend a careers fair in the local market town. No one from the trade stands approached me. I could not understand then that a neurotypical world places so much biased emphasis on the appearance and the visual. I was a spotty, slightly overweight, ungainly youth gazing woefully at the light seeping around the door, wanting to run and escape from this room flooded with too loud and too numerous conversations.

Before leaving for fresh air and a quieter sound stage, I passed a stand for the Royal Air Force (RAF). An officer in a serge blue uniform thrust a brightly coloured glossy leaflet towards me. I looked down at it. It was a technicolour avionics festival of swooping aircraft and highly engineered technology. I looked back at the officer. He smiled at me and asked if I liked aircraft. I think I gave a noncommittal shrug. Not to be put off, he asked me what subjects I was good at. I told him geography and history. Did I like exploring and learning, he asked. Did I like travelling? Yes, I did – on my bike and on the train. Would I like to go further afield to see other countries? Yes, I suppose I would, I replied to him in a vague manner.

'Well, you could do much worse than join up, young man.'

'Join up.' The phrase confused me. What did that mean? He asked me about my hobbies. I said I liked reading and, oh yes, I liked hi-fi systems, I liked to hear sound as if it was real.

'You like electronics?'

'Yes,' I said, 'I have assembled and built a radio from a kit. It works.'

'Great!' he replied, then enthused, 'We need young men like you!'

I took the leaflet and politely thanked him for his time. I said I did not want to join today, but I may consider it.

'No, we wouldn't expect you to sign now! Anyway, you are too young at the moment, and you'd need to talk it over with your parents.' He looked at the badge on my school blazer. 'You are at a good school. You'll probably want to go to university first. We run bursaries to help fund that. There is a number on the leaflet if and when you need some more information. Don't forget...'

## Hurting again

A wave of panic struck. I looked at the suggested timetable that my tutor had handed to me one morning. If I was to get the projected grades, he explained, I would need to study every night for at least three hours, and at least one of the two days of the weekend. No downtime, no bike rides, no walks, no exploring and no leisure reading. Certainly no pleasure or escape.

As well as the panic and gut-wrenching fear that I had experienced previously, it was now supplemented by something else, thoughts that I was unfamiliar with. A sense of gloom. A darkness, like the sun would never, ever shine again. Forever swamped behind a stubborn dark cloud, I remained trapped on an ever-revolving wheel of school, studying and classroom. Hemmed in, in my bedroom at home, I became isolated and my mood deteriorated. My mum and dad said that it would end, that the examinations would be over, and that we had a wonderful summer holiday to look forward to in the Lake District. I thought that I would be fine after the exams, and I solely focused on that with tremendous effort to block out the overwhelming desire to give up and escape.

One day had three examinations alone, English literature, applied mathematics (part one) – a gruelling three-hour exam – and, worst of all for me, French (oral). My mood deteriorated at home. I became snappy and distinctly unfriendly. My mum blamed teenage hormones. I started to hate myself, and my cosy little world felt fractured. In between exams, I broke down in tears in my room, with French phrase books and French grammar textbooks and novels written in French scattered around me.

However, it ended before June did. The weather improved and warmed up. School was over and I had the family holiday to look forward to. I had not been to the Lake District before, and the thought of exploring some of its geology and landscape heartened me.

Exams were finished, at least for another two years, and I had put much distance between myself and what I thought was the source of my troubles. But these fears and emotions had now become completely separated from the actual source of my troubles. They weren't in the classroom, or in my bedroom while studying, they were inside me, inside my head alone. I could not make any sense of this. I could not communicate what I was going through to my parents. What would I say to them? I could not articulate it to myself. I did not know the word depression then, and I had no idea that many other people were experiencing the same feelings as me right at that same moment.

## Welcome to the world of work

The economy in the early 1980s was not buoyant. The decade had started with an economic recession, and graduate unemployment was very high. My parents, wanting the best for me, said I could spend three or four years at Keele University or elsewhere, but have no job or any money at the end of it. I had set my heart on geography as being the hub of any form of working by this time, so I struggled to see any other path. I went to the cinema with my friend and there was an advertisement for the Royal Air Force. I remembered the careers fair. There was an Armed Forces office in the city that we were in. After the film, I tentatively stepped inside. I mumbled something about electronics and trade training to the sergeant behind the desk. He eyed me up and asked about my qualifications and what I was doing now. He said I could attend a college, within the RAF, and be paid to attend, and go on to have a guaranteed well-paid job, as well as having civilian electronics qualifications. I could also do a degree through the Open University, which the RAF would go some way to pay for. While this all sounded sensible, there was an important question. Was I prepared to kill someone, a stranger, if someone told me to do so? He also asked me some rudimentary fitness questions and said that I needed to lose some weight, although he did not see these as insurmountable obstacles.

I left school on Friday afternoon, and on the following Sunday morning I was on a train heading up to Lincolnshire and into a completely new experience. The routine was necessarily hard, the cold morning starts were brutally early, and the other recruits were from very different backgrounds and classes compared to my pro- tected grammar school. I was not used to the wave of profanity and ribbing and banter and the unnecessary, to me at least, cruel and crude humour, both from the recruits and the non-commissioned officers. Banter is something I can never understand. To this day, I cannot see the point. A lot of the comments thrown at me hurt. They did not like the number of examinations that I had passed (only a few of us were going on to 'Radio School' as it was so termed), they did not like my lack of accent and perceived public school voice, and the way I precisely phrased everything. But worse than this was the homesickness. Although I had been away from home before, I had never felt anything so deep-rooted, the feeling of being so unutterably out of my depth. I struggled with things that required deft manual dexterity, like bed packs and stripping down a rifle at speed.

I spoke to our barrack room corporal, the same one who shout- ed at me for my bad posture and for 'tic-tocking' (being out of sync with the other paraders due to my innate poor co-ordination). I explained the homesickness, and he nodded sympathetically. I said I could not cope with this, and I could not see myself doing this for years (I had signed up for nine years' service). He said, in an understanding tone, that it was all a game, that they were trying to weed out the weak ones. He explained that once I started Radio School things would be very different, indeed not that different to being back at school. He said the shouting was not to be taken personally and it would be fine as long as I went along with my superiors and did as I was told. He said not to consider leaving in the first few weeks, as I would regret it later in life, and that I would look back on these six weeks with fondness – something which has *not* turned out to be true. I gritted my teeth and got on with it, but not without real physical effects, as my irritable bowel syndrome, which I have to this day, kicked in and my body was washing food through me, leaving my resistance low.

I passed out of basic training and went on to Radio School, but the initial training had taken its toll. I was washed out and went down with gastroenteritis. I was in the sick quarters for over two weeks. It felt like being in solitary confinement, and my electronic studies fell behind. I recovered, and somehow caught up with my studies, and my confidence grew back. The corporal was right, on this point at least.

Two years later, I was a fully fledged radar technician. The years passed, and I finished my service career on a clifftop in Cornwall solely looking after a (then) very state-of-the-art piece of kit.

I did my job well, and although I was known to be aloof and somewhat unsocial (in that I did not go out much or do the dreaded b word), my quirks were tolerated to a greater degree because of my job proficiency.

## The first fall

After completing my nine years' service, I went to work for the manufacturer that made the radar system that I worked on. It meant a move (I had married by this time and my wife was pregnant) from the South West of England to the depths of East Anglia.

The imminent arrival of our baby filled me with more mixed emotions. I find this really difficult to write, but I am still ashamed to say that when my son was born my immediate first selfish thought was to commit suicide. I was in the maternity hospital, and straight after the birth, at which I was present, I headed towards the exit to get some air. On the way to the exit there was a large winding staircase and I stood at the top of the stairs and seriously contemplated throwing myself off. I stood there for several minutes. I thought of our hopeless financial situation. We were in private rented accommodation, which took a large slice of my pay each month, but my salary was comparatively small and my wife did not work, something which was now unlikely to change. I intensely disliked my factory-bound job. I did not have the innate skills to be a father. I had not attended father classes, not that I was ever aware that there were any. I did not know what my new role was to be. We were both a long way from our own respective families. I was out of my depth, and I could not see a way out. I had never had suicidal thoughts previously, and, at that moment, I did not have the outside insight to observe or rationalize my own thoughts.

A nurse passed the staircase, and saw my introspective looks and my pallor. She asked if I was okay and I replied that I was not. She took me into a side room and got me a cup of tea. I told her what I had intended to do. She did not show any shock, but added that paternal depression was more common than people realized, but people seldom talked about it. She said that she would tell no one else but strongly recommended that I speak to my own GP as soon as possible.

A couple of days later, while the midwife was with my wife and child at home, I was sat in front of my GP, an elderly Asian man, whom I had not met before. I found it distinctly odd to be talking to a stranger about the thoughts going on in my head. He was kindly and understanding and prescribed me something I had not heard of previously. He also signed me off work for two weeks. I later learned that the anti-depressants were of the MAOI (monoamine oxidase inhibitor) types, which had greater side-effects than the later SSRI (selective serotonin reuptake inhibitor) types. No counselling was offered, but he wanted to see me in two weeks before I returned to work. He also gave me a card with the Samaritans number on it, together with an emergency NHS mental health line number. He said too that he would need to advise the midwifery and ancillary team due to the seriousness of having suicidal thoughts, but my wife would not be told.

I tolerated the anti-depressants for four weeks, the job another six months. Nine months after leaving Cornwall, we were back again.

## The second fall

I was successful in securing a managerial position with a well-known former high street department store retailer. After six months, I was given my own store, one of the fastest promotions the company had ever had. My new store did well, sales were up, customer service feedback positive, and I self-started a number of Head Office projects alongside it. I was promoted again, to a large store in Oxfordshire, but this time my wife did not come with me. I commuted the 270 miles every weekend, staying in digs during the week. This took a toll on my family life, but our income increased and we finally bought our own home.

My wife wrote to the regional director, unbeknownst to me. They met me in my store saying that my wife was unwell, and in the interests of all, they would arrange for a move back to Cornwall.

I was sent to a similar-sized store, but instead of the good working relations I had had with the team in Oxfordshire, I had an immediate personality clash with the assistant manager. One night, I had left clear and concise instructions as to what work I wanted the late evening shift to do, as we had a district manager visiting the next day. When I got in the next day, none of the things that I had asked to be done had been, not one. In addition, some of the moves went completely against the Head Office rules, and I knew that our imminent district manager's visit would be a complete travesty. To my shame, I verbally flew at the assistant manager. We had a huge row in my office, where she stood against my door, blocking my own exit. In retrospect, although I did not understand it at the time, I was having a classic autistic meltdown. I pushed the manager out of the way, and ran down the steps to the outside of the building deliberately throwing the store's keys away with me as I left.

I knew I had done wrong. I knew I had completely overreacted and behaved badly. I drove miles away to a place where I knew I would be safe. I was wrong, very wrong.

It was classic Cornish mining territory, complete with tin mine engine houses, with the iconic granite chimneys dotting the landscape. It also was replete with exposed mine shafts. I stood over one of the shafts and looked down into the gaping, cavernous hole. The world behind and around me blurred and went out of focus. I could only see the hole and its depths. I had thrown in the towel with my career. I had worked hard for several years for nothing at all. I would not get a reference, I would be out of work, and, most importantly, we as a family would be homeless. It was all so hopeless.

I stood there for a very long time. Minutes melded into hours. I could no longer feel my body and any rational thought had long disappeared. Self-killing my useless brain seemed the only way out. It had not provided me with any fullfilling happiness, and made me struggle with every little thing. I pushed my toes upwards, like a diver on a board, and arched my body...

'You alright, mate? Say, you okay?'

I could hear footsteps getting closer, but I did not look around. The hole was engulfing me.

The footsteps grew louder and faster and I felt something around my waist.

'You don't want to do that mate, it ain't worth it. They ain't worth it. You are worth more. Look, I'm gonna get some help. Come and sit down over here and look at this view instead.'

He pulled me back. This stranger had broken the thought train. He sat me down on a rock a few feet away. Another walker with a dog was nearby. He told this second stranger to sit with me while he got help. He explained that he had a carphone in his Land Rover. Not long after that I was being taken to the cells in Camborne Police Station, because no suitable NHS hospital accommodation was available. I was in there for 24 hours, and the only help I was offered was a brief chat with the duty psychologist.

Luckily, I did not lose my job, or our home. I was given some help, and I got to see a psychologist. I was downgraded as part of the disciplinary process, but I was still a store manager, albeit in a smaller store. I stuck it out for another two years, keeping myself buoyant on anti-depressants and exercise. I was, surprisingly, head-hunted by another retailer and moved across to them, in a nearby market town. The challenges of working in retail for me remained. I was good at the planning, organizing and managerial side, much less so at the people and direct customer skills, although, again, my new store began to perform well.

## The third fall...and a diagnosis

Two years after being in my store, the anti-depressants that I had been on for four years stopped being so effective, and the depressive gloom re-emerged. My brain became more sluggish, and I struggled to do the simplest of tasks. The mound of paperwork in my in-tray stayed there as I ceased to function as an employee. The inevitable happened, and I was signed off again from work, initially for one month. My employer was keen for me to return to work at the earliest opportunity, so they paid for me to see a private counsellor who adopted some innovative (to me) techniques. This included a process known as rewind therapy. He also wrote a (personal) letter to my GP, who subsequently invited me in for an appointment. The GP referred me to a private clinical psychologist, for reasons that were not made clear at the time. After a six-month wait, I travelled to the psychologist's own private residence. After three meetings, and access to my school records and other medical files, he diagnosed me with autism (Asperger Type, AQ 44/50). This news was not a tremendous shock. I was already familiar with Asperger's syndrome as my son had been diagnosed with it some ten years previously. The diagnosis explained the things I had found difficult in my life to that point, and I knew that depression and anxiety were co-morbid with the condition.

I returned to work and settled back down, but it was still not to be an easy path. The slow slide with all retail had begun, and the axe fell on my staffing budget. We still had to achieve the same stretching sales targets and customer service, but now with considerably fewer staff. Because I was on an annual salary, I was finding that I had to personally plug the gaps, because my overtime was unpaid. I started sleeping in the store, as I found it necessary to stock the shelves myself after the store had closed in the evening. I started self-harming by cutting my arm with a pair of scissors. I began to get panic attacks to a paralysing degree. As well as taking a toll on my health, it also caused irreparable damage to my family life and marriage.

I was signed off sick again, but this time I did not return. After 18 months, my employer cancelled my employment contract. I was unemployed now without a family home. The entire experience and trauma meant that I could not return to a professional career, and, to this day, it has left deep scars, emotionally, with self-confidence sapped and with my mental agility and memory permanently weakened.

## Helping

### Helping therapies

Between episodes of acute depression, and during each recovery phase, there has been a succession of things that I turn to for comfort. Some of these do not help directly with recovery, but do assist with day-to-day coping and the management of everyday activities.

One of these is my radio. My head is a constant chatter of noise and nagging self-voices, telling me of things I need to do, or things that I should have done, or, more usually, done better. The worst times of the day for me are mornings. If I am having a particularly deep depressive episode, listening to the radio is a source of both comfort and distraction. I am not talking about music at this point, but speech radio, be it news, discussions, phone-ins, documentaries or comedy, and especially drama, which acts to shut down my inner voice and enable me to focus on something else which is not involved with my own personal life. It is a technique I have used since my teenage days, and sometimes helps with restless sleepless nights as well. I find radio more involving than television; the latter now seems to cause more sensory overload as I get older, and I no longer derive the pleasure from it that I used to. However, I do enjoy cinema (as long as the cinema is not too busy – mid-week afternoons are usually ideal) and find the immersive escape of a great, well-written and well-acted story perfect.

Music is another comfort to me, although I have to be in the right mood, and the choice of music is often critical. Headphones combined with music shut out unwanted extraneous sounds, and can lift my mood or take me into a different plane altogether. I do get a bit fixated on sonic fidelity, as my hearing is hypersensitive, so things like production and mix of the music can be as important as the music, and lyrics if there are any, as well. I have a wide scope of musical styles that I listen to and would encourage anyone to listen to other genres outside their normal preferred choice. For example, for years I shunned jazz, but now I find the syncopation and freestyle liberating, and the complex rhythms can be a pleasure to follow, like trying to track a maze.

A general point about help is that much of what I am writing about here is not limited to autistic people. There is a wave of mental health problems sweeping our planet, and it is beyond the scope of this piece to discuss the reasons for that here. However, I would like to say that the things I have found useful to survive can apply to anyone experiencing depression and anxiety, as well as things like obsessive compulsive disorder (OCD) and hearing voices. This links into mindfulness; I have attended NHS-funded courses, and while I was the only (known) autistic person on the course, the techniques (which can be adapted to suit your own needs) have helped me in more recent times. A particular mindfulness technique I still use is the 30-minute body scan. A quiet warm space is essential to begin, and a soft mat to lie down on. I use a CD track downloaded onto my mobile and listen on earphones where a therapist talks me through the practice, focusing on my breathing and all parts of my body in turn, while excluding (or trying to exclude) all extraneous and random thoughts. I do feel liberated and refreshed afterwards, and it can improve the quality of my sleep, both depth and duration.

Reading throughout the years has been very beneficial to me. It is akin to a mindful technique where the process of scanning the written word and converting it into a story with real characters, and using creativity, or non-fiction, where I am enriching my knowledge of the world, is a soporific and beautifully relaxing experience. With fiction, I feel that I can step inside the world that the author has created. Unfortunately, if I am feeling particularly down or overwhelmed, for example after a shift at work, I cannot process the words and they tend to blur together, or I am unable to follow the strands of the story, and end up re-reading the same paragraph over and over again, which can add to my low mood. That aside, I always allow time in my week for reading, usually before I go to work after I have had breakfast (I get up early, as it is a quiet time in the household). I feel lost if I have not spent some time reading, and I truly feel it has added a very important element to my total life experience. I also like to be surrounded by books and enjoy browsing bookshops, both new and secondhand. The tactile sensation of turning pages, and the smell of both new and old paper, is part of the process of reading for me. Reading from screen, while better than not reading, has a more limited and less immersive appeal.

When I was explaining my hurting experiences, one of the things I said in passing that I found beneficial was nature and being absorbed in the natural landscape. Urban areas do the complete opposite. The pace of life, the noise, the speed of people and traffic and the sheer mind energy (in dodging people and their eye contact and shutting out extraneous noise) that I have to expend on walking along a very busy pavement make cities and large towns places that I shun, unless it is absolutely essential. I have a personal belief, not scientifically based, that it is the massive expansion of urban living over the past 50 years that is resulting in greater mental health problems across the globe. Therefore, for most of my life I have been lucky enough to live in rural areas, or in places that have easy access to the countryside, so that I can escape into a safe, reassuring environment.

Why is the green space so important to me, and what pleasure do I derive from it? Well, first, it comes back to that sonic space, the timbre of rustic noises, the sounds of birds, of trees rustling, of grass lilting in the wind, which all have a therapeutic effect on my mind. I tend to visualize things through my ears more than my eyes. It both transports me from threats and reassures me by lowering my anxiety. The almost complete absence of people and the hazards that they pose to my well-being is a boon. Walking within a natural environment soothes my inner soul, as well as being beneficial on a physical level (exercise and fresh air), raising my endorphins. The pure rhythm of putting one leg in front of the other while absorbing sonic beauty is a mindful process. By concentrating on my breathing, I can reduce my heart rate, as well as improve my mood. I am also absorbed and fascinated by landscapes. I love the sun tracking across the sky, casting shadows and shapes over the undulating fields and the visual cadence that this produces. The green forms and the reddish hue of the soil where I live both contrast and play with each other in a delightful visual ballet. I cannot get any of this free therapy from an urban environment. The second point about green spaces is that discovering something new in nature, a rare flower, a scarce bird, an unusual mineral, both educates and delights my synapses. It enriches me in a way that, say, a modern piece of architecture or a shopping mall cannot. Being absorbed in this rural moment, casting aside and throwing away working trauma, makes my life, albeit transitorily, seem worth living.

Endorphins are released by the pituitary gland during exercise as a response to perceived pain by the body. This hormone release has a feel-good effect on brain mood and is a natural effective method of reducing depression. The amount of exercise does not really matter, as long as it is aerobic (getting the lungs and heart to work faster than they do while sitting) and sustainable over a 30-minute or more period. Workouts that are too intensive can have a reverse effect, so a case of less is more over a regular period is likely to bear a better result. For me, I have been running, on and off, since doing cross-country at school some 42 years ago. I have had some issues with my back and have had to give running up for periods of time. I now find doing various forms of activities in the gym as beneficial as going out for a full run. Particularly of benefit to me is rowing. I think this is because of the rhythm and hypnotic effect which transports me away from darker brain imagery. When combined with earbuds shutting out extraneous sounds inside the gym and music at the right tempo for rowing is selected, the overall effect can be tremendous. Any form of group or team-playing sport is counter-productive as the added stress of social situations undoes any derived benefit.

Another beneficial exercise for me is swimming. I find the whole swimming process, dare I say, immersive, but not just in the physical sense. The weightlessness feeling when in the water is liberating, and it gives me an enormous sense of freedom that simply cannot be had anywhere else. As well as being physically beneficial, it has an enormous positive effect on my mental well-being.

Choosing hobbies and exercises that you both enjoy and derive value from is the essential part. Everyone will have their own best form of escape, their own best way of dealing with a neurotypical world, be it computer games, Lego, chess, diving, golf – it does not matter as long as you enjoy it and you feel that your body and mind are deriving benefit.

Two other techniques I have found beneficial are yoga and breathing exercises. This is not the place to expand on yoga practices, suffice to say it is worth trying yoga at least once to see if it is right for you. I find it liberating and it has the added benefit of stretching muscles and keeping joints supple.

Breathing exercises do not need any special equipment, any trainers or educational manuals. I employ this simple method when I am feeling particularly overwhelmed or over-stressed. Find a quiet, peaceful corner (or plug in some earbuds or noise-cancelling headphones) where you will not be distracted for a few moments. Sit or crouch down. Breathe in deeply and slowly, hold for a second, then breathe out again slowly. Slowly focus on the breathing, and try to shun away all other thoughts aside from the process of breathing. Continue until you feel calm again.

### Rewind therapy

During my third fall, and just before I received my autism

diagnosis, a counsellor that I went to see, who was funded by my then employer, practised a technique called rewind therapy. Of particular benefit to anyone who has suffered serious trauma, like a car accident, or a painful, emotional incident, it is a simple technique. The counselled person is placed into a near-hypnotic restful state where they recount their historical trauma. This trauma is then relived, but then repeated at a more distant adjunct, like imagining viewing it on a television screen, then in black and white, then more slowly, until finally it becomes a more dim and distant memory. It does not eradicate the memory, but it enables the brain to process the trauma in a less emotional and more practical manner. Following this technique, it is possible to move forward and develop plans for the future. It may not work for everyone, but if you have had trauma, and have problems with post-traumatic stress disorder (PTSD), it might be worth seeking out a good quality, testimonial-backed counsellor.

In my case, the trauma was the three previous breakdowns caused, essentially, by work and working conditions. Although it did not resolve the issues with my employment, it made me understand myself better as a person. Up until that point, anything in the future felt completely unconquerable.

It was this same counsellor who wrote to my GP suggesting that I see a clinical psychologist, as he had picked up on my autistic traits. For that, I owe this counsellor a tremendous amount.

## Helping treatments

I have seen many counsellors, as well as psychologists and psychiatrists, since my first fall, some better than others. Some of these NHS counsellors and psychologists have used cognitive behaviour therapy (CBT) with me (and sometimes as part of a group) with somewhat mixed results. CBT can be very effective, but, particularly with autistic individuals such as me, the method, and the person delivering the method, is paramount to any potential benefits. One of the sessions I have had is dealing with anxiety, a common source of problems to autistic folk such as me. I still have anxiety issues, sometimes to an acute and paralysing degree, so in that regard you could say it has not worked. However, possibly my anxiety would be worse and more disabling if I had not had CBT. It is a very difficult thing to measure, and cannot be captured as easily as NHS post-counselling questionnaires would have you believe. On balance, I would say if you have not had CBT before and it is offered to you, grab the opportunity with both hands and go into each session with an open mind.

That said, counselling and CBT has its drawbacks, and in particular early sessions can be traumatizing as previous bad experiences are relived. This can raise the possibility of suicidal thoughts or self-harm. It is well worth being alert to this, and having telephone numbers for support groups like the Samaritans close to hand. CBT requires commitment and there is often homework in the form of workbooks or diaries to complete. If the counselled person is not committed to these processes then the CBT will simply not work.

Having a rapport, a mutual understanding, with the counsellor is also vital. If the sessions are not working for you it may be worth trying another counsellor. Some have been trained (but not nearly enough) to counsel autistics, and if you can find one who has been accordingly trained, so much the better.

I have not taken sertraline or any SSRIs for a few years now. Although they have been a real help to me in the past, and I keep a standby supply around the apartment for those 'just in case times',

I have been using a herbal-based medication as a replacement for sertraline. This is 5-HTP (or 5-hydroxytryptophan), a naturally occurring amino acid. It is commonly produced from extraction of the *Griffonia simplicifolia* climbing shrub commonly found in West Africa. I must emphasize that it should NEVER be taken in conjunction with a SSRI as the serious serotonin syndrome can occur, which can be fatal. However, it is a useful substitute for SSRIs. I would not recommend taking it without seeking a GP's advice first, and for someone experiencing a crisis I would suggest that SSRIs are better.

The benefits of 5-HTP are that you can stop taking it without withdrawal symptoms, and you may well find that the side-effects are fewer than they are with SSRIs. However, it does come with some fairly mild side-effects of its own, including mild stomach upset and stomach ache. This usually goes after the first three or four weeks. It does help with both depression and anxiety as well as OCD control. It is non-addictive and can be readily purchased over the counter in most health food shops in the UK. It does work best with B vitamin supplements (sometimes the tablets already include this) or you can take a separate multi-vitamin and mineral supplement.

## Helping friends and family

I owe much to my parents for their love and support, bringing me into this world and their sage advice. This still continues, as I battle through a turbulent neurotypical world. They have been there for me throughout my breakdowns and troubled periods without work.

I have had few true friends throughout my life, but they know who they are and they have been there for me. Sadly, my best friend who I cycled with regularly passed away in 2002. This hurt me terribly.

My wife too is an enormous support, and I am very lucky to have her to support me.

It is very difficult to do anything about a situation if you do not have friends and family around to support you, but I have found the autism community on Twitter to be both supportive and a useful source of information. You may find an autism support group near you; these are often excellent and a good place to source advice on employment and benefits.

I find the workplace difficult at all times, and rarely have I struck up a friendship with someone at work. It is such a social minefield, for which I do not have the accompanying manual of hidden codes, that, in my opinion, it is best avoided in terms of a support network.

## Time

Time is still a major issue for me. I find that it takes me longer to get ready to go out than the so-called average person, as I have to plan everything, and anything manual, due to my poor dexterity, can considerably slow me down. As we live in a majorly neurotypical world, the clock seems to be permanently set against us, and time measurement tends to be in the negative. Time is the most difficult thing to battle against – be it work targets, or life milestones, it is always working against me. Most time targets seem superficial to me, but, despite telling myself this, it seems to make a scant difference to my anxious state.

Apart from planning, and managing my time as best I can, and attending numerous time-management courses, I still find this part of my life a significant and troubling handicap. I do not have any easy answers for this part of my life except to say that as I get older I tend to care less about it, with all the ramifications that brings. I tend to just accept things for what they are.

## Hoping

I write this last closing section on hoping in interesting times. It is the spring of 2020. I am fortunate to live in a beautiful, idyllic part of England, and the weather is gorgeous, but the planet is going through deeply strange times. A new coronavirus hit the Northern Chinese province of Wuhan in late 2019, and as I write this we have already had over 120,000 deaths from this virus in the UK. I work as a key worker in a supermarket, therefore I continue to work, providing food on the shelves for the local community. The strange and frightening situation, working on the supposed frontline, has heightened my anxiety levels, and it has meant I have had to revert to SSRIs in order to keep working during lockdown and being surrounded by shoppers, any one of whom could be contaminated with the virus.

However, it is not as grim as it first appears. There is hope. Global carbon dioxide levels have plummeted. Nature has taken back empty town centres. People seem kinder. A lot of good work is being done in our communities. As well as a focus on the virus itself, there is a lot of focus on mental health, and those who are struggling. There is a renewed assessment of benefit levels and how realistic they are, now that more people are having to rely on them.

Right now, despite having increased anxiety levels, along with the greater proportion of the human race, I have hope for the future. I am lucky, I feel fortunate. I have a wife, a roof over my head, and I have paid employment, and that job is being recognized as important. I no longer feel like a mere shelf-stacker. I am being thanked by customers for coming to work. Despite anxiety, I feel hopeful for the future. I am able to keep in contact with family virtually, and we are able to walk from home within beautiful, rustic, jewelled landscapes.

My future seems more buoyant somehow, and I am able to reconnect with my creative side again. I have started writing again. Over the past ten years or so, I have written four novels and I have a fifth that I am working on. The current environment seems the right time to do this. My mental state, for years at odds with the majority, now seems in touch with everyone else's. I am still hopeful that these novels, with something important to say in an entertaining envelope, will reach a wider audience.

I am more hopeful for mankind. Although it will be some time before the effects of the pandemic leave us, this time has given us pointers to how all mankind can live in a more sustainable, peaceful and meaningful way. I am at peace with myself, and I truly hope that after you have read this, you will be able to take away some nugget which will enable you to live at ease, and to maybe furnish yourself with a more comfortable autistic life.

# Feeling Alien in a World That Rejects You

## The Discovery of Self Through Neurodiversity

SUZY ROWLAND

## Hurt

When you emerge from the darkness, the world is new, unfamiliar. The pain your body has endured is so complete, your re-introduction into the world of friends, family and familiar surroundings feels like a rebirth. I remember a colleague remarking to me, 'You walk round as if you have a dark cloud over your head', in recognition of my depression, without calling it out. The depression 'cumulus' is visible to everyone apart from the person over whose head it hovers. Traumatic memories hovered on the edge of my consciousness, and their intensity didn't get in the way of my daily life. But becoming a mother can shake even the strongest emotional constitution. Becoming a mother of a neurodiverse child demands a resolve most of us didn't even know existed.

I was born in the urban Midlands, about a hundred miles away from London, and my upbringing was modest, humdrum even. My mother, who became a single parent when I was seven, worked day and night – literally – to keep a roof over our heads. Well spoken and ambitious, my mother was a Jamaican immigrant, who came to the UK in the 1950s. After I was born, she went to night-school to train to be a teacher and was promoted to become a curriculum adviser, picking up a master's degree on the way. She was passionate about the opportunities education afforded to 'ethnic minorities' as a means out of poverty, even aspiring to the middle-class life. Hard work and good behaviour were her watchwords. A child of Jamaican heritage in 1970s Birmingham, I couldn't hide my difference. I tried to adopt a local 'Brummie' accent and a zany chatter to cover my shyness. I couldn't understand why I generated so much attention just by being me.

I went to university, which gave me the space to explore my own dreams. Rather than the constraints of academia, my passion was to work in the creative industries. I dreamed about being a writer, a TV presenter, a poet, a painter. After graduating, I sought employment in London, enjoying a colourful succession of posts in magazine and book publishing. Life was good, I continued to enjoy an exciting corporate career, and was financially secure enough to bring up a child alone when I fell pregnant. Ten years later, when I was expecting my second child, I knew how to play the game of life. I had overcome many hurdles and discrimination in the mainly white world of my work. I had stuck my neck out to raise both of my children alone.

With no prior knowledge of autism, I had no reason to suspect my son was on the spectrum, although my first call about his behaviour came from the nursery when he was just two years old. The nursery manager wanted to talk to me about Lucas's lack of interest in playing with the other toddlers and his difficulty in following instructions; more worryingly, she voiced concerns about his behaviour and rages. I remember that phone call distinctly; it was when the first spots of 'mother shame' began to take hold in my mind. Our health visitor referred him to a speech and language therapist for group sessions when he was about three, to correct some speech anomalies. The speech therapy was a benign intervention and didn't seem to be connected with his nursery behaviours, which may have precipitated an assessment and diagnosis, but no one was looking for autism, so he started primary school wide-eyed and vulnerable.

Starting primary school is a big event for all children, but if we consider the well-documented stress impacts of transition on neurodiverse brains, the events that followed as he strove to fit into his busy mainstream primary classroom were inevitable and upsetting. There were incidents of bullying, accidents, gentle enquiring concerns from his two class teachers but no hint of further investigation. His reports spoke of a kind, helpful little boy who was meeting learning targets but was underperforming in social and play metrics. 'Falls below the standard that would be expected in a child of his age' was how the teachers described his social skills and abilities to work with other children, collaborate and co-operate.

The 'incident on the pirate ship', where Lucas fell or was pushed, was the last straw; no one seemed to know or have seen what happened, but I had already decided to find another school. It wasn't the panacea we were expecting. His new school managed his emotional dysregulation through a variety of harsh and punitive reactions, including exclusions, as I recorded in my book *S.E.N.D. in the Clowns* (p.151):

Exclusions were the soundtrack to Lucas's primary education.

The many years of exclusions before he was diagnosed with ASD [autism spectrum disorder] and ADHD created a child who was on edge, defensive and sometimes explosive in pressurised situations. He described the feeling before a meltdown as a volcano, which he couldn't always control. By the time he got to secondary school his generalized anxiety led to a range of mental health difficulties and he was consumed with his 'failure', which was dimming the light of his lovely personality.[36]

By the time Lucas was six, he was at school number three and still undiagnosed. The strain of constantly needing to be alert, worrying where the next school 'bomb' was coming from, was wearing us down. I wrote this poem through one of my darker days:

*Low Mood*
Scraping inside for the light
Scraping around for what's right
Feeling my way in the dark
Not knowing where is the start
Feeling the weight on my back
With worries my mind starts to crack
Knotted with tension and dread
My head groans and guides me to bed
Sleep comes, at last I am free
To soar, to fly freely, be me
My dreams are delicious with meaning
As they playfully bounce from the ceiling
Sooner than time I'm awake
A new day I must undertake.

Although Lucas attended school cheerfully every day, the cracks were beginning to make holes in his demeanour. He developed the shrug of a child who is often chastised, unsure of themselves, nervous, trying to please, confused and doesn't trust the adults around them. Childhood trauma can refer to serious one-off events like abuse, bereavement, domestic violence, war, natural disasters. But when we are notching up adverse childhood experiences (ACEs), many parents are unaware that the constant worry about their child at school – have they had an 'incident', accident, are they being bullied, punished, will they be excluded? – over time may even become an ACE. These cumulative ACEs amount to trauma. These prolonged 'low-level' traumatic events are every bit as impactful on a child and a family's mental ill-health as major events. From a psychological perspective, when children exist in a perpetual state of fear and uncertainty, their building block of emotional well-being – their sense of safety – is weakened, which can lead to long-term damage to emotional well-being and feelings of negative self-worth. Research studies have shown that children who experience early childhood trauma, abuse or neglect are more likely to go on to develop profound and long-lasting mental health problems in adulthood, such as 'complex PTSD'.[37] This is a difficult area to unravel as so many of the causes and effects are interconnected. Additionally, the impact of abuse or neglect varies from child to child and these are influenced by a host of external factors as well as the individual's level of resilience. For an autistic child, who may see themselves as the cause of everyone's ire, there seems to be no escape, as they're unable to escape from themselves. Once we realize the extent of the damage inflicted on young lives who have experienced discrimination or been misunderstood, it's imperative that, as a society, we provide every help and encouragement for that young person to heal and in time become proud of who they are and learn to feel comfortable in their own skin.

You can't see the damage happening; to the outside world it may look like you're 'coping', but the longer the turbulence continues, the deeper the loss of self-worth.

The teachers' end of the day reports were increasingly unsympathetic; my heart rate peaked as I pulled up by the school playground each morning. I was often late for work as I needed time to calm down after the veiled threats from the teachers and my over-the-top begging for Lucas to have a 'good day'. Anxiety and nervous tension appear in the body in strange ways. Some of us bite fingernails or twist hair, others blink rapidly or click pen tops repeatedly. When the adrenaline is coursing through your body, it needs an outlet, which is why so many holistic practitioners recommend yoga or mindful activities to still your racing mind. But if your racing mind needs to perform in a work environment or go home to look after other children, or care for an elderly relative, how and when do you have time to re-group? Inevitably, that anxious energy is turned in on yourself in possibly harmful ways or will transfer itself in every one of your subsequent interactions. If an unresolved problem follows you around in this way, it's natural to come to the conclusion that you are the cause of the problem.

Many studies show that living alone significantly impairs mental health.[38] Single parents who live as the sole adult in their dwelling are particularly vulnerable if they are caring for dependants, and there is no one to talk to about their worries.[39] I didn't acknowledge my own emotional vulnerability and ploughed through each day feeling battle worn.

Lucas was at his fourth primary school aged almost nine when we got his diagnosis of autism and ADHD. Like many parents, my feelings were a mix of shock and relief. Some parents said afterwards, didn't you know, you must have had an idea? I didn't. It was a Year 2 teacher who had first mentioned the autism word to me, but she left before we had time to talk in more detail. On reflection, his difficulties highlighted a neurodiverse profile, but with no experience of this in our family, it wasn't a consideration to me. I have no idea what Lucas felt, he was so used to being derided, excluded, disenfranchised and disciplined; he had become a shadow of the smiley infant he used to be. Although there were many opportunities to assess him, his ongoing issues were viewed as a social, emotional and parenting problem – that is, a presumptive analysis that supported a pre-existing bias. Increasingly research indicates that a lag in diagnosis is common for young black autistic children,[30] which is detrimental to the young people and their families due to the absence of appropriate early intervention (often cited as best practice for autistic developmental and academic outcomes).[40] There are other barriers that black autistic boys face, for example the symptoms frequently observed such as hyperactivity, behavioural difficulties and emotional dysregulation lead some clinicians to diagnose ADHD instead of ASD.[30] We had a dual diagnosis.

In other examples, non-compliance related to transitional change or non-compliance in a particular lesson or activity may lead to a diagnosis of oppositional-defiant disorder.[30] The pattern of delayed and missed ASD diagnosis may be prevalent in children of the black diaspora, and while I hesitate to describe the negative reactions I experienced with class teachers and headteachers as racism (I understand that teachers are not trained to diagnose), I assert the belief that value judgements come into play when children from a specific cultural background or demographic are in dialogue with authority figures in education. If teachers are not trained to counsel or diagnose, it's vital that children are seen by compassionate and representative experts, early in this process, to avoid baking in negative and cyclical exchanges. How many youngsters remain 'invisible' to potential help-providers, because their hidden disability remains resolutely unidentified behind an avalanche of hyper visible assumptions?

A colleague, Clare Ward of Special Networks,[41] summarizes this perfectly:

> People from Black African, Caribbean, Asian and many other cultures are underrepresented in service providers and over-represented in mental health service users. Somewhere in the middle are people of colour who are autistic. 'The minoritied minority from the missed generation'. Only by listening to some very raw stories can we begin to understand. Only by having these conversations can we bring about a very necessary change.
>
> @maskoffcampaign

My appraisal of myself was of a bright black executive in a white corporate world, an ambitious woman and mother, who happened to have Caribbean heritage. It seemed others' appraisal of me was quite different: black single parent, failing parent of black child. I found myself curling back into my childhood insecurities of not fitting in at school as parents of Jamaican immigrants. I was living a duality, where my corporate self was a million miles away from my mummy self, but the holes in the mattress were starting to show. Maybe disclosure was the answer? I shared with my line manager some of the difficulties I was having with my son at school. I instantly regretted it; she became morbidly interested in what was going on and now I had told her there was nowhere to hide. When the headteacher called me at work for an urgent meeting about my son's behaviour (*Yes, I know it's difficult to manage, but what can I do if I'm at work?* I thought), it was getting harder to hide my feelings; my body language was betraying me. I was sinking into a dark box of confusion and my son was tumbling in behind me. I turned in on myself, endeavouring to explore my predicament through poetry. The following rhetorical words were the beginning of my mind starting to process, throwing out some ribbons of reason:

**Drive by**
Trees and fields flashing by
Dark illuminates the sky
You are the night
You are the road
You are the lorry's heavy load
Miles are passing
Petrol gauge low
You haven't actually moved at all
Your foot hits the floor
Your panic rises
Heavy rain lashes the windscreen and cries
'Why can't you see me, why oh why?'
Is it the darkness
Or is it the cold
'Just let me into your arms to hold!'
The wind creeps under the chassis and screams
Why are you scared of the night and your dreams?
Losing the grip of reality's bite
You come face to face with your fear of the night.

## Help

The beauty and irony about finding help to heal your hurt is realizing that the help was there the whole time. But you didn't see it, you simply were not ready for the warm blanket of recovery. It can be frustrating for outsiders – who may even be in your own family – to see you suffering needlessly but unable to reach for help when it is offered. After a disastrous transition to secondary school and my son then being out of school for almost a year, it wasn't possible for me to stay on at work. I needed to be at home with my son, and put the time to good use by studying ASD and ADHD, psychology and also cognitive behaviour therapy before eventually setting up the #happyinschool project.[42] As a therapist, I refer to the 'healing window', the stage between acknowledging that you are struggling and not feeling ready to accept outside help and knowing that you do need additional people and tools to help you emerge from the fog. Everyone knows when they've reached the point for help – it can't be forced. If you wait too long the healing window can close, leaving you feeling that 'no one can help me and I'm better off left alone'. Human beings need time to absorb and understand their emotions, it's a cognitive process, which differs between people.

Neurodiverse individuals don't necessarily process pain and hurt in the same way as neurotypicals, who can use 'talk therapy' for example. Once we had the diagnoses, we had turned an emotional corner, but we had to heal from the pain of the bumps and bruises of a difficult decade. The transition to secondary school didn't go well, and was followed by another school move. At his second high school, work began in earnest to find the channel for Lucas's 'hard to articulate' emotions and for him to process some of the rejection and chronically low self-esteem that had built up over the years. We were a long way from self-actualization and pride in being neurodiverse, but we were peering through the healing window. It was time to get help.

Both my son and I found comfort in the creative space – his was art and drawing, mine was poetry and writing. Lucas began to balance out some of his more extreme mood swings and spent a mostly happy and productive three years in his final secondary school. The build-up to public exams came fast, probably before either of us were ready. Thankfully before and during this turbulent pre- and post-diagnosis season, Lucas had regularly attended a community arts-based project called Knots Arts,[43] which I'd found through our local chapter of the National Autistic Society.[44] Being part of this group was a fantastic creative and safe place for help. I've always loved drama and the performing arts, having trod the boards at London's Bloomsbury Theatre in my youth. I figured a drama-based programme wouldn't feel too much like a 'heavy' intervention for Lucas, but filling in the application form brought home to me the realities of his condition. I was asked to rate his behaviour across a number of situations and describe the activities that would calm him down in the event of high emotional overwhelm. Somewhere in small writing, they mentioned about reserving the right to withdraw places for young people who were unable to be successfully regulated in the sessions.

We passed the trial session when he was eight and he still attends eight years later. The strapline for Knots Arts is 'untangling social knots', and this is done so gently with the young people, they don't even notice because they're having such a good time! It usually starts with 'circle time' where the young people share their news of the week – good and bad – and reflect on that with the others. To start with, some of them are reticent about talking out loud in front of their peers. There are barely whispered voices, lots of twisting and squirming in seats, maybe a sentence or two, with no elaboration. I observed a few sessions at the start and we noticed how difficult Lucas found it to talk about his week; he would often miss out huge chunks of good news, such as passing a guitar exam, and talk instead about tiny detail or just say that 'nothing had really happened'. We used to rehearse what he would say in the car, so he could participate. They played age-appropriate games, which were skilfully woven together with social exchange, information sharing and teamwork. Their annual Christmas plays are a consistently high standard of performance which showcase the various talents of the group. During term time, however, when the children are in the midst of functioning at school and trying to push through their difficulties, I see them shining but raw. Some of them have eating disorders, some hold their bodies in the exaggerated tension of not wanting to be noticed but knowing that their very being creates attention. The young people wear some of the badges of intense mental anguish: restrictive food intake, self-injury, school avoidance. Anxiety loves company, which makes it difficult for parents to be relaxed about food intake when shopping for and preparing food for the whole family seem to dominate the week. Many of the parents looked stressed and tired and it became clear that the drama group wasn't just help for our children, but the two hours per week they played and shared was respite for us too. I used to browse the shops for the two hours' duration of the club, then became more interested in talking to other parents, but conversations didn't always flow. Many were locked in their own hurt of managing their child's moods, dealing with school issues or the general exhaustion of trying to understand why it was difficult for teachers are other health or care professionals to listen and help in the way they wanted them to.

One of the group leaders asked me whether my son had processing issues. No one at school had asked me that before – most of the investigations related to school that focused on his needs were either punitive or corrective. I was surprised to be asked about his cognitive challenges. It transpired that his processing speed was slower than his neurotypical peers, especially in free-flowing conversations. He needed more time to understand a question he was asked, formulate a response and find the right words he wanted to answer. This analysis was confirmed later after a detailed diagnostic assessment with a clinical psychologist.

Our next help came in human form, the sort of warm and inspiring human being you want in your corner when your world is turning upside down and you don't recognize anything about your life anymore. She was the educational psychologist called into Lucas's first secondary school to investigate his behaviours in the classroom. I only had one or two meetings with her in which she seemed to utilize all of her diplomacy skills. She'd completed the classroom observation and it was during the presentation of her report that we met for the second time. She paraphrased her report, carefully explaining that Lucas's behaviours appeared more exaggerated in a school environment that had high expectations of conformity and strict behavioural standards. Unfortunately, the school leadership were resistant to her recommendation for whole school autism training, because it was at odds with the school's disciplinary policies. She also highlighted the positive aspects of Lucas's personality and explained the sorts of situations that could be causing him to overload: the noisy classroom, his need for processing time and his lack of understanding around the complexities in pre-teen social interaction. She summarized that Lucas would be able to thrive in the school, but he would need significant adaptations from the school leaders. I felt a flicker of hope in her words, but something was off key. Lucas's class teacher and head of year weren't in the meeting. She calmly explained that the school leadership had shown little interest in investing in such training.

Many parents go for the 'smaller class sizes' option for their autistic young person without intellectual disability, in the hope of providing the best chance of academic success. It's a logical thought process, but one that can be inherently flawed. The child may be highly capable, but their intellectual ability may be blunted by an environment that's too inflexible. In addition, a school may be ignorant about the nuances of that individual child's autism. Having smaller class sizes does not automatically mean that the classroom will be quiet and non-stimulating, or that the teaching staff will be overly concerned with the child's well-being in favour of the school's academic results. It's a bitter pill, and the hardest part to swallow is the acknowledgement that the amount of money invested doesn't always equate to the best quality of care or the right sort of therapeutic support. It's a lesson we learned fast. Some families invest hugely in time and effort to squeeze their neurodivergent child into a learning environment that doesn't fit. We all flourish when we feel nurtured and respected; it's an ideology I strongly support when considering the competing emotional and academic needs of the talented autistic young people I've encountered, including my son.

## Hope

My late mother's name was Hope. Dorcas Hope Walker. Her whole life was the embodiment of hope. For a better future, a good career for her daughter and granddaughter, the reduction of racial discrimination towards most of her school community. She lived and breathed history (English and Caribbean), she loved the ballet and Radio 4. But as hopeful as she was, she didn't understand my son's autism. She hoped he would learn to behave. As a devout Catholic she hoped and prayed his Catholic school would provide what he needed. It didn't. Like many carers, my mental health declined while taking care of her in her declining years. Her traditional Jamaican culture didn't equip her to understand his neurodiversity. My hope is that within my son's generation, 'elders' of all cultures will grow to accept neurodiversity and more broadly mental ill-health in their communities and their own families without ostracism. It is my hope that neurodiversity is more clearly understood in school communities, which should theoretically be safe spaces for young people to discuss divergence of all kinds. There is a pressing need for all mainstream schools to ensure that neuro-different children are positively engaged in their school communities and that their peers receive age-appropriate neurodiverse and cultural education. We need to make faster progress in dismantling some of the harmful societal misunderstandings that create anxiety and other forms of low self-image in our autistic youngsters. I found myself grieving for my mother in the same year that my son's assessment and diagnosis was completed. I dedicated my first collection of poetry 'Songs of My Soul' to this highly emotional part of my life's timeline.

My son is high-functioning autistic; this used to be known as Asperger's syndrome. His intricate mind, and that of other young souls who are on the autism spectrum, needs to be free to fly. There is much we need to learn about the mysteries of the autistic mind.

And many more people who need to understand what autism looks like in its many forms.

While there is much to be done, I'm encouraged that there are many vibrant people and platforms shooting up that are empowering autistic children and their families, delivering workshops, sharing information and positive success stories. Black, Caribbean, African and dual heritage autistic families are sharing and networking, charities are moving away from the medical model of autism into a more social model, which looks at difference as well as commonalities. The mindfulness movement is being adopted by mainstream schools, the Mindfulness in Schools Project (MISP),[45] specialist teachers are honing their well-being practice, with more and better strategies available to all pupils, which are particularly helpful for autistic pupils. This excites me and gives me hope.

Since my son's autism, ADHD diagnosis, I've immersed myself in autism and neurodiverse theory and engagement and, in this space, I have found hope for humanity. I see similarities between groups of people who have been hurt and damaged for simply being themselves: transgender, non-binary, queer, black and so on, many of whom are also neurodivergent. There is bravery in speaking about your experiences, as it puts a spotlight on you. Not speaking about your experiences means no dialogue, which in turn means no increased understanding, which slows down the opportunity for progress. Through my son's diagnosis, I've changed my career, devoured new and old neurodiverse literature and own voices literature. Through a sense of loneliness and a need to fill a void in a pressured hectic life, because I was alone with two dependent young people, I found a new life through a difficult experience.

The change has been complete and all-consuming. Reading snippets of other people's stories and classic texts by Lorna Wing,[46]

Steve Silberman,[47] Temple Grandin[48] and many others helped me to feel connected to a new way of being. It's a world I inhabit through my work, but it has also flung open the doors of my life to new colleagues, friends and experiences. I'm joining the dots between school exclusions, poor mental health, social exclusions and limited future employment prospects for specific groups: black children of Caribbean heritage and autistic and ADHD youngsters, and those who straddle both camps. While there is a lot of information available on social media about autism and ADHD, parents need to do a lot of work to find what they need. I felt compelled to pull together a body of research findings, parental anecdotes, alongside my experiences to provide useful context and strategies to enable the families I meet to feel knowledgeable and encouraged. I wanted to take the academic language and make it universal and accessible for autistic families of all cultures; it felt important to empathize as well as answer some of the key questions parents ask in the pre- and post-diagnosis stages.

While looking through the lenses of research and clinical evaluations, the real joy for me is talking to parents and their autistic children and knowing that I can breathe the hope of my experience into them, touch them, and emote with them in a personal way that highlights the positive human elements of standing up for difference, standing strong for equality. I want autistic people to read this book and feel recognized, validated and part of the whole community. It's how I longed to feel as a dual-heritage citizen looking into a society I felt alienated from. My work has demonstrated to me the effectiveness of informed advocacy as a key link to break the chain of long-ingrained biases and misinterpretations around many forms of discrimination. All discrimination stems from ignorance and fear. Both require change-makers to ask difficult questions and be willing to listen to the answers. I am particularly interested in barriers to diagnostic equality in all areas of mental and physical health. The National Autistic Society (NAS) says, 'Autism is not a mental health condition, but many autistic people develop separate mental health issues. Often this can stem from a lack of appropriate support.'[49] NAS invites the question of how many people are detained under the Mental Health Act who have undiagnosed autism or ADHD as a key presenting need, creating a subsequent mental health condition. Psychologists are in almost total agreement that child behaviours are nearly always functional in origin.[50] It seems that autism and ADHD can be missed in certain groups of boys, if the function of their explosive behaviour is viewed as attention-seeking or disruptive. It's acknowledged that girls are underdiagnosed with autism, as they present so differently from boys, but what is less discussed is the rate to which black or black mixed children, in particular boys, are left behind in this diagnosis lottery.

I feel a deep connectedness to the parents who attend my #happyinschool sessions, a great sense of personal and collective achievement that I am able to share something so personal that provides a service to others. I have discovered my own voice and found spiritual and emotional freedom and huge job satisfaction, where I'm able to use my corporate skills in a more compassionate environment.

Autistic children and their families are speaking more and being heard by academics and policy-makers in their requirement for equality and social justice, and this gives me the most hope of all. I discovered my own advocacy voice during the diagnosis and changing schools' phase. I could see how neurodiverse kids experience similar negative attention, discrimination and ignorance that I experienced as a brown child in a mainly white school. Going through the diagnosis and school process opened my eyes to the sad reality that discrimination and poor understanding of autism and ADHD isn't just about kids being mean to kids. As I wrote in my book *S.E.N.D. in the Clowns* (p.58),[36] 'Early intervention is the key to preventing some of the unnecessary stress autistic children, young people and their families face, such as long wait times for appointments and inappropriate support or needs not being met.'

I'm fascinated by the concept of masking for acceptance, both as a successful survival strategy but also as a cause of deep damage to the psyche by loss of your true identity. Is the mask hiding a true identity or presenting a new, stronger identity, behind which the more sensitive personality can safely hide? I see my younger self in many neurodiverse children. I see her pain and joy. Although I'm not a teacher like my mother or my daughter, I teach my own brand of hope.

### Who am I?

Somewhere deep in life
if you're lucky enough to live that long

you happen on the great opening up
heavily disguised as the great shutting down

suddenly nothing works
because everything works perfectly

your broken relationships
are the parts of you that hurt

your place in the world
is bigger than the scope of your vision

your inner sermon implores you not to speak
but to listen

everything works because you have thrown away
your clothes of falsehood
to stand naked in front of the world.

# To Be Left Alone

EMMA WISHART

## My childhood

I was always a very strange child and was aware from as early as I can remember that I was different from everyone else. I had a terrible reputation as a troublemaker and was seen as very stubborn, rebellious and disobedient. The truth is that I often did not understand the instructions or requests I had been given. To be clear – I was not unintelligent – my reading level was far above the other children in my class. I had understood the words but not the way they were used, the extra or different meanings implied by the adults and seemingly understood by the other children. When I tried to defend myself for my 'disobedience', saying 'but you said...', I was accused of being cheeky, answering back, being pedantic or purposely obtuse. Nobody considered for a second that I could have genuinely misunderstood – after all, I was clearly extremely intelligent. I became so wary of 'answering back' (as it was called) that I became scared of answering any questions at all and got in trouble for that too. I remember even as a small child feeling that there was something vitally important that had been told to everyone except me, or that everyone else must have psychic powers and I had been left out. The sense of isolation among a group of people was overwhelming and I was only ever happy when I was on my own.

Unfortunately, it is not possible to be alone all the time and school had to be endured. Children have an unerring ability to single out the child who can be mercilessly bullied and wound up. I used to utterly dread break times and do my best to make myself invisible. This didn't often work and as a result I was constantly in trouble for fighting in the playground. It is noteworthy that nobody ever got into trouble for fighting with me.

When I went to secondary school everything changed. It was a girls' school and a 'good' school, so there was no more physical violence, but the mental cruelty continued. Reading my school reports it is clear that the teachers didn't know what to make of me – a clearly very intelligent child whose academic abilities were extremely erratic and who showed no effort or interest whatsoever in subjects she didn't understand or didn't see the point of, yet was able to (seemingly) effortlessly pass exams when she needed to. I was described as 'aloof' by one teacher, and the underlying theme is that they did not at all understand anything about me. There are also several disparaging comments about my appearance and the condition of my clothes which were never addressed at the time, to my knowledge.

So, it continued, with any achievements I made being belittled or dismissed and any faults being blown up out of all proportion. I felt that I was utterly unacceptable and that my personality was being forcibly ground down or squashed out. Gradually I learned to be a pretend-normal person, learned correct responses and reactions, but the concentration required to navigate even brief conversations left me constantly exhausted.

## My teenage years

When I was 14, I reached crisis point and made a very genuine attempt to kill myself. I was utterly devastated to wake up and find that it hadn't worked. I couldn't even do that right! Of course, the hospital ticked their boxes by referring me to a child psychologist but clearly he too didn't know what to make of me and I only saw him a couple of times and he never made any further appointments. The school put it down to attention-seeking behaviour and I was on the receiving end of some very severe lectures from teachers about how naughty and selfish I had been, particularly as I could have exacerbated my mother's illness (heart condition). I was made to feel, if possible, even more insignificant, and particularly now I was aware that there was no escape.

I sought escape in other ways, becoming obsessed with music and collecting records. I had three paper-rounds and a weekend job and must have spent hundreds of pounds and amassed an enormous collection of records (or vinyl, as it is now known!). I joined an evangelical church, which horrified my parents, but I left after the whole group, including the leaders, laughed long and hard at me for sharing what I thought was an interesting piece of information. So, then I turned to cannabis, which in truth didn't really seem to affect me at all but made me appear to fit in. This involvement resulted in my parents getting so angry with me that they forgot they were not supposed to hit me in the face. It was a very normal occurrence for them to use violence on me, but they were usually careful to ensure that no marks were left visible to others. Sporting the resulting bruises at school culminated in me being removed from my parents' house and placed with a family of a much older girl at the school who habitually took in foreign students. I do not believe that social services were involved as, to my knowledge, I never spoke to a social worker. I believe it was done 'on the quiet' so as not to damage the reputation of the school.

Looking back on my school years I find it inconceivable that people chose to believe I was wilfully being different, rebellious and purposely choosing not to fit in, making myself miserable in order to make some kind of point.

So, at 16, after my O-levels were finished, I was on my own. I got a temping job in an office and rented a room in a shared house, student-style. I moved four times that year due to falling out with the people I shared the kitchen and bathroom with, and the same thing kept happening until I was 19 and found a self-contained flat I could afford to rent. At last, after eight moves in a couple of years, my own space! It was bliss and I stayed there for two and a half years. All this time I had been doing temporary office jobs with two brief periods of being employed by places where I had previously temped because they liked how well I worked. But once we got to know each other it all went wrong, and I left to go back to temping. I was starting to notice that I seemed to bring out the worst in otherwise quite nice people, a theme that would only get much worse as I got older.

## Being a grown-up

When I was 22, I decided I wanted to buy a house, so I accepted the permanent job that my current temporary placement was offering me and bought a three-bedroom terraced house. Now I was, of course, trapped in a way that I hadn't been when I was renting, but I was determined to be a proper grown-up and meet my responsibilities. Luckily I was employed at an institution that had many different departments and their practice was to move all the employees around periodically, so every time my manager and I fell out irretrievably they were able to pass me on to someone else. I managed to remain employed there for almost seven years, my record!

When I was 29 things between me and my manager started to seriously deteriorate. She picked on me constantly and mercilessly and I was hauled in for disciplinary meetings on an almost weekly basis. Any attempt to find out what I was accused of or to defend myself was only taken as proof of guilt and used as further ammunition against me. I was called stubborn, rude, unco-operative, inflexible, facetious, pedantic, difficult, awkward – in short, I had an attitude problem. At appraisal time, I was always told that my work was really excellent but that my relations with others were unsatisfactory, so I always got a bad overall report. I couldn't understand why I was doing so badly when my work was such a high standard, and I thought that that was what I was there for. One day there were several extremely stressful factors at work which were pushing me to breaking point but, on top of this, my manager decided that this was the day she was going to ride me ragged about having forgotten to wear my name badge. Despite explaining that I had left it at home she kept insisting that I put it on, relentlessly and endlessly, even pursuing me outdoors when I went to get some air and try and cool down. I completely lost it and left, never to return (although I didn't know that at the time, of course). I was signed off sick by the doctor with 'nervous exhaustion and depression' but now I know that this was autistic burnout.

I was signed off monthly and for the first couple of months I had assumed that the doctor would stop certifying me at some point and I would have to go back. But, and I consider this to be l moment in my life, for one appointment my doctor was not there and I saw a different doctor in the practice. I was fully expecting to have to go back to work but I walked in and before I even said anything she was full of empathy and sympathy with how awful and scared I was feeling and signed me off for another month. This changed my way of thinking and I started to try and think of a way to escape.

I knew I had to do something radical to ensure that I was never trapped in such a situation again. Step one was to ensure that I did not need lots of money in order to live and to attempt to live on benefits. I had visited a friend in west Wales and had noticed that property was much cheaper than the south of England. Thanks to the disproportionate increase in property prices I had a bit of equity in my house and I decided to find a house in Wales that I could afford to buy without needing a mortgage. I found only three houses I could afford that were not squashed up in town centres with other houses. One wasn't finished and I had neither the money or the know-how to fit a kitchen or bathroom, and one had a tenant with lots of dogs who made me feel very guilty about potentially making her move out and have to find another rental property that would take her dogs. In retrospect, this would have been the more suitable property for me, but being a people-pleaser, I could not evict this woman.

I bought the remaining property, an 18th-century cottage desperately in need of renovation but habitable, just. It was semi-detached but the other cottage was completely derelict, so I thought I would be safe from neighbours.

## Moving to Wales

So, I commenced what I hoped would be a peaceful life in the countryside, but it didn't really turn out that way. The road outside the house turned out to be something of a race track despite the 30mph limit, and because the house had been empty for so long it was assumed that my parking space on the forecourt was public property and chapel-goers parked there blocking me in. My idyllic idea of life on unemployment benefit became very unpleasant when it became apparent that the women in the dole office were not going to stand for my laziness and obstinacy in refusing to apply for all the outrageously unsuitable jobs they thought I should be applying for. I did apply for a lot but perhaps luckily for me I am absolutely terrible at interviews and was fairly safe from actually getting one. Even so, going to sign on every fortnight was a nightmare and filled me with dread. The women in the dole office were exactly the sort of people I was trying to avoid by not working, and I hated that they held so much power over me.

I attended an interview for a part-time job in a mail-order bookshop which was only five minutes from my house and actually got the job, to my surprise. I think that this was the first and only time I had got a job from an interview. Later I discovered that only two people applied and the other one had not turned up.

It all went very well at first; the part-time work allowed me time to recharge myself between shifts, but they soon demanded more hours from me when they realized what good value for money I gave. Of course, I could have said no, but I didn't (and still don't) believe that my wants or needs carried any weight. In fact, I have come to find it easier to give in to what other people want me to do than have to have an argument and still end up doing what they want.

Again, autistic burnout threatened, and as my nerves became more fragile, I became a target for unpleasantness. Again, I seemed to bring out the worst in someone who was not a bad person. This culminated in a vile verbal torrent of hatred one day, full of really personal insults; this person must have been bottling up all these things for ages to have exploded in such a dramatic fashion. In a way reminiscent of the last time this happened, this woman also pursued me, this time to my house where she walked up and down outside the windows for some time and repeatedly knocked on the door. Later I went to the managers and reported what had happened and they agreed that what she had said was true and that she was perfectly justified in saying it! Needless to say, I found my position there untenable and asked for six-months' unpaid leave to go away and think about things. This was refused, so I had no option but to leave.

## Running away again

I went to New Zealand for six months and spent most of the time camping out in the bush, sleeping in my car, completely alone, only venturing near a town if I needed food.

When I got back I still wasn't sure what to do and went on the dole again for six months but got to the point where going to sign on was causing really severe anxiety and distress and I simply had to think of another way to live. In the meantime, someone had bought the derelict cottage next to mine and was doing it up, so there was no peace there.

The only place I had had any peace was the New Zealand bush, so off I went back there again for three months. I realized that that was what I needed – no house and to be in nature. It was while I was sitting in a forest by Lake Hawea that I decided that when I got home, I would sell my house, buy a campervan and live in that. I reckoned that my house should be worth enough that I would be able to live on the interest of the money, therefore not needing a job or benefits, as long as I only wanted vital necessities.

I came back to the UK and briefly drove around and lived in a campervan.

While driving around I had noticed signs at the side of the road saying 'Woodland for sale' and I decided to investigate the possibility of buying a plot. Eventually I found one that matched all my criteria.

## Living in the woods

So began 12 years of living in the woods. This was exactly what I needed, and it was an extremely healing experience. I was almost entirely left alone with a few exceptions; it was a small plot in a much larger area of woodland, so there were other owners who would occasionally drop by when they were visiting their plot, and one other person lived in theirs full time too. However, he was about as far away as you could get and he quickly got the message that I did not appreciate him dropping in at all hours and had not moved to a wood in order to find companionship!

I had to arrange for ways to become more self-sufficient and rigged up a rainwater collection system. I bought a solar panel to charge my phone. It quickly became apparent that winters were going to be extremely difficult, if not impossible, to cope with, so

I fell back on my usual plan – go to New Zealand for the winters where, of course, they are having summer.

During this time people kept telling me how brave I was and how much they admired my intrepid spirit, which I did not understand, because the reason I had ended up in a wood was due to running away from situations that I didn't know how to handle. I think that bravery is not just doing something that someone else finds scary, it is being scared of doing something and still doing it. I did explain this but nobody understood or believed me and I have since learned that because people mean so very little of what they say, they attribute the same to me and assume that I don't mean what I say. This is disappointing as when I say something, I have usually thought about it very seriously and weighed it up and come to a serious decision.

During this time, I had started to notice that I always fell out with people and seemed able to bring out the very worst in otherwise quite nice people. I started to wonder if it could be me, or something about me, particularly as at my last job I had asked why I had to obey a different set of rules to everyone else and they had said, 'We don't know, but you do. It's just you, we don't know what it is, but it is something.' I researched the possibility of personality disorders, mental illness and everything else I could find that might explain it. I certainly fitted a lot of criteria for many conditions but none of them was exactly right until I discovered autism. I knew immediately that this was me and set about trying to get a formal diagnosis. This was 2006 and it turned out that there were no facilities for adult diagnosis and my doctor knew absolutely nothing about autism, what it was or what to do about it. Nonetheless, I now had a name for what was different about me.

## Diagnosis autism

I had not been to the dentist since I was 19 and I had lost a filling when I was 25. When I was 43, in 2013, this tooth became infected and I got a large abscess. I tried to treat it with home remedies for about a month but realized I needed medical attention when I woke up one day with my whole head and neck swollen and feeling feverish. Reluctantly I made a doctor's appointment and got some antibiotics, but while I was there the doctor saw on my notes that I had requested an autism diagnosis seven years previously. I had given up on it but it seemed there was now a service for adult diagnosis and she asked me if I wanted to be referred, so I said yes.

It took several months to get the first, pre-diagnostic interview and it was just over two years from that doctor's appointment that I finally got my diagnosis, in May 2015. I was 45 and suddenly I wasn't just a mad person living in the woods anymore, I was autistic.

Getting a diagnosis is a real rollercoaster of an experience. I had to come to terms with a whole new way of thinking about myself with respect to other people. It has been likened to watching a film with an extremely unpredictable plot twist, and then watching the film again knowing what is going to happen and seeing everything in that new light, with a new understanding. You can account for things that seemed impossible to understand before and slowly things begin to make more sense. This is a process though, and takes time to work through; it is similar to the stages of grieving, in a way. I had to say goodbye to the person I had been trying to be all my life and become a new me, hopefully a more authentic me. But in order to be your authentic self you need a loving, supportive network of people who accept you and your diagnosis and this is not often possible for the person who has been masking their difficulties and camouflaging themselves to fit in throughout their whole life. People see that I have always done it and 'seemed fine' and don't understand why I can't continue to do so. They do not understand the enormous mental strain and gargantuan effort that goes into every single interaction and do not see me having to hide myself away for days after any social activity or a day at work. I worked two days a week and spent the other five recovering and I know that people did not believe me when I said I hadn't left my flat, or hadn't spoken to anyone, since I last saw them.

In addition to my difficulties not being accepted by people I see regularly, my family also do not see that my diagnosis should make any difference to them, but they all live far away and I do not often see them.

I have a few good friends, most of whom are autistic but a few non-autistics who are very accepting. It is not necessary for us to see each other often and indeed we can go for months without any contact and then pick up as if no time has passed. There are no judgements, just support, acceptance and gentle encouragement when required. In order to complete the process of fully becoming my authentic autistic self I do feel that it is necessary to break off contact with people who do not accept how difficult interactions with them are for me. The chronic people-pleasing side of me is wrestling with this as none of them are bad people, they are just too busy to listen, or they think they already know all about it, or what I am telling them doesn't agree with what they think they know about me.

Something that I find extremely difficult to explain is how I choose what to do in my spare time. People try and persuade me to do things or go to things because they think I will enjoy them and won't accept it when I say I would not like to do them or going to them would cause me distress. I understand that there are a lot of people who can't bear to be alone even for short periods of time, and would rather be with absolutely anybody, anybody at all, than be alone. I am the exact polar opposite; I would much rather be alone than spend time with anyone whose company I did not actively enjoy. I enjoy being alone so much that there are very few people I like spending time with. People seem to think this is a bit sad and that I must be lonely. They ask me, 'But what do you do on your own all day?', as if they can't imagine somebody existing without someone being with them. My personal opinion is that I think it is a bit sad that people have to be with someone whose company they don't enjoy much because it's better than being alone with themselves.

I did ask a few people why they thought I was living in a tent and I had responses such as 'To be rebellious', 'To be close to nature', 'To be eco-friendly', 'Because you don't like being indoors', 'Because you like camping'. Sometimes I tried to explain that I felt I had been driven to it as the last possible option of staying alive, but people really couldn't grasp this concept. Interestingly nobody who knew me ever asked me why I was living like that – they all assumed they knew – 'Oh it's just Emma on her latest crazy thing!' One time someone who didn't know me asked, which made me think about what to say. Actually, he asked me if I had chosen to live that way and I said, 'Well. Say there's a box of chocolates. Someone says you can choose any chocolate you want. Ah, oh, not that one. Not that one either. Oh no, you can't have that one. And in fact, the only one that's left that you are allowed to choose is the marzipan one and you really want a chocolate, so you choose it. Have you really chosen it? The alternative is not to have a chocolate at all.' Needless to say, we did not become friends, but I was proud of the analogy.

## Destination Milford Haven

Once I was diagnosed, I set about trying to improve my life, starting with moving indoors. It was lovely living in the middle of the wood, but I was getting to an age where my bones and joints were suffering in the cold and damp, and even before I started the diagnostic process I had decided to try and sort something out for when I turned 50, and then revised this down to 47 after the next winter. Also, no longer having a vehicle and living two miles (with many hills) from the nearest shops was taking a toll as I had to cycle to get my shopping and could only get what I could carry on my back. I applied for PIP (Personal Independence Payment) and for the tiny amount of pension I had earned working for seven years in one place. It took months for it all to come through but in October 2015 I was able to move into a rented flat.

It was a lovely flat and I was very lucky to be able to move in as they normally only allowed 'professionals' to live there. Obviously, I did not disclose at that stage that I was in fact homeless and gave them the address of a friend that I had been using for post, pretending I had been lodging there for ten years! (I have come clean now and the letting agent knows the whole story.)

While it was very nice and an extremely high-quality flat, it was on the bottom floor of the block and I was aware that there must be an outstanding view of the sea from higher up, so I asked that if a flat higher up became available, I could have first refusal. How monstrously lucky I was then, because one of the two penthouse flats became available for only a tiny bit more money. I signed up and paid over the deposit without even viewing it and it was the best thing I have ever done. It is a gorgeous flat with the most amazing view.

I wake up every day and am so grateful and feel so lucky to live somewhere so lovely. I cannot imagine living anywhere else, despite the fact that it is in a town, which surprises everyone who knows me given my previous bucolic existence! My answer to this is that when you have had to cycle four miles up hills to get shopping, being able to pop out for milk is the greatest luxury of all.

## Autism awareness to autism acceptance

I became involved with a charity who wanted me to write and read out a very short account of my life as part of an awareness course about learning disabilities which had an hour of autism awareness at the end. I was terrified, mortified and horrified but with help I managed to write a short piece (probably only about two minutes' long) and read it out to some local police officers and social workers as part of their training. I was so scared and almost in tears at my sad story and had to keep reassuring my listeners that there was a happy ending! I delivered this a few times and the overwhelming feedback was that these people wanted to know more about autism, so it was decided that a full-day's course on autism awareness would be written and me and a couple of others would tell our stories as part of that. Many months went by and it gradually became apparent that nobody who wasn't autistic actually knew anything about autism without a learning disability, beyond the usual stereotypes, and they were absolutely at a loss as to how to go about writing a course on it. During this time, I had been asked to speak at other functions and had written a much longer and more detailed version of my story which I had delivered a few times. I was gaining in confidence that people actually wanted to hear what I had to say, which was entirely a novelty to me.

I decided that I would have a go at writing the course. I started researching as much as possible, talking to and listening to other autistic people and finding out what exactly it is that we want to tell the world. I quickly discovered that 'awareness' on its own was of absolutely no use without acceptance and understanding. I then deviated from the basic brief of 'autism awareness course' to a course which would help people understand why we do the things we do and why we think the way we think. I had to pick apart stereotypical views of autism propagated by so-called experts and explain the true position. The end result was a course that the autistic people I have shown it to heartily endorse but I have been assured that other people find offensive. I do not see a way that I can explain what it is like to be autistic without also giving ideas as to how to help us, so a stalemate has been reached.

## Hope

When I was 14, I honestly, genuinely and truly wished to end my life because I had no hope that I was wanted or that there was anything for me. I can feel afraid of hope because if you hope for something that doesn't happen the disappointment can be crushing. I was afraid to be let down again.

But I have a naturally optimistic disposition and always try to look for the best in a situation, or ways to solve things instead of only complaining about them. As this story reveals, I have been treated appallingly badly by many people, usually before it was known that I was autistic. In a few instances, I have been treated badly by people after I'd told them that I was autistic. Sadly, they didn't understand or care to find out what that actually meant for me or their interactions with me. My reason for sharing my story is not to be self-indulgent and I am not looking for sympathy. My aim in sharing these experiences is to show how some people seem to think it's fine to treat autistic people (even if they don't know they are autistic) really badly.

In my next project, I will be exploring what some of the reasons for this might be. I have written a full-length autobiography describing a lot more of the things that happened to me, and some of the outrageously dangerous things I have done, and why.

It is called '*But You Said...?!*' *A Story of Confusion Caused by Growing Up as an Undiagnosed Autistic Person*, and it is available from Amazon on Kindle and in paperback.[51]

My hope in doing this is to increase understanding and therefore acceptance of the differences that autistic people have in our ways of thinking and how this translates in our communication and behaviour. I have written about many of the co-occurring and often misdiagnosed (or missed altogether) conditions that often come with autism and how they affect me and some of my friends. If I can cause someone to stop and think about what they are doing and perhaps, for a moment, think about what the other person is experiencing before chastising, humiliating, punishing or abusing them, then I will be very satisfied.

The ideal future that I hope for would be that everyone will be appreciated for their uniqueness and gifts instead of being labelled as dysfunctional and deficient. People will be accepted for who they are instead of being forced to conform to societal norms and ostracized if they fail. People will be encouraged to have jobs suited to their skills and be allowed to flourish in comfortable surroundings. I have so much hope that people sharing their personal stories will help to achieve this. We need to make autism personal, show that we are people, give it a human face. Autistic people seem to me to be somewhat dehumanized in the media.

I felt I was an abject failure as a flawed neurotypical person. But as an autistic person I am sincerely hoping that I will be able to make a difference and help other autistic people.

# Being Autistic and Managing Anxiety

ROBERT JOYCE

## Anxiety is hurt

Alexthymia is something that occurs in some autistic people. It is the phenomenon of being unable to describe feelings and emotions – to understand that you are experiencing something, but are unable to communicate what that is, both to yourself and others. As I am autistic, alexthymia is something that sometimes happens to me. Often I get asked the question 'How are you feeling?' and I find it almost impossible to answer. Yes, I am feeling something. It's there. A sensation in my stomach or chest. A sense of further questions arising out of this simple one. Uncertainty about what is happening to me as my mental and physical self responds to the query. However, there is one emotion that I always know. One feeling that it is impossible to be confused about.

Anxiety. It is like an old enemy. It's always been there. The feeling of unease, panic, stress, worry. Whatever word I use, it all sums up feeling uncomfortable within myself. I have always experienced it. I cannot remember a day in my life where I have not felt anxious at some point. I can distract myself with movies, books, hobbies, events and so on, but I can never eradicate it completely. I can only manage it. And I guess I do, although it is sometimes hard to believe that.

Anxiety is not a diagnostic trait of being autistic but sometimes I think it should be. For me, the two are linked. Autism and anxiety. Anxiety and autism. I was diagnosed quite late in life at the age of 38, and as an autistic adult I have reflected on my past to discover who I am. The question of why I am so anxious has come up many times. My autistic mind works overtime. I always over-think everything and a single thought can generate a hundred questions. Often these questions have no answer. Just take a minute to think about that. Have a question in your mind, anything, and imagine that you must answer that question or some unknown bad event will happen. Now imagine that question, for whatever reason, has no answer. Does that feel stressful? Is there any sense of panic?

That is how anxiety can feel for me. Each thought and question creates unease, that can build and build until I feel lousy. Plus, this is not just mental. Anxiety can grow to a level where I experience physical symptoms: feeling sick, upset stomach, feeling like I want to urinate but can't, joints ache from feeling tense and I experience fluttering within my chest or sometimes headaches. This can then add to the worry further. For example, is my stomach upset because I'm just nervous or is it actually that I am not well?

Anxiety has affected the way that I have lived my life. When I was a child the worry would be one of the factors that would stop me playing with other children (the other being my lack of social communication skills – a key aspect of autism). I was worried that I would get hurt by them or that there would be some sort of trouble. When I started school, it was just the same, although school was worse because the social and sensory factors of autism added to the anxiety.

As I got older and school became a source of learning more interesting material, my anxiety also developed. I think the main anxiety I felt was a fear of failure. I wanted to be top of everything and excel at every subject. For example, during maths, I would strive not only to answer the questions set to me, but as many as I could from the textbook. In English, my essays would be written over and over again to get them right and would be pages too long. For science, religious studies, geography, history, all my notebooks were full of extra material, such as illustrations that were not really required. All my free time outside school was filled up with extra work so that I could be the best.

Why? Because I was worried that if I did not do all this, if I wasn't the best, then nobody would like me. My parents wouldn't care about me, I would be a failure. This anxiety is one of the deepest rooted throughout my life. The need to succeed and receive praise was overwhelming. It also meant that I missed out on doing other childish pursuits during this time. I engaged less with people and spent my valuable time striving to get those A grades. More importantly, the feelings of needing approval and the fear of failure has been so deeply engraved into me that it has affected my entire life. I still strive for that praise and those grades to this day. The problem is they are easily attainable while you are at school, but in adult life there is nothing. Nobody cares much about such things and this adds to the daily feelings of anxiety.

I then reached my exam years and discussions were had about my future. I stayed on to do A-levels but there was no chance I was going to university. I remember thinking about it and being scared of leaving home and not coping with the workload. The workload was an irrational thought, since every essay I had ever written at school was the length of a dissertation. I never knew how or when to stop. The problem of leaving home was more rational. The worry of being able to look after myself, to fit in with other people and to be so far away from what I knew was overwhelming. I did not know it at the time, but this was the fear of change which haunts so many autistic people.

I felt that I could go, because my mind was academic in nature, but then it was impossible as I was just so scared. I buried my anxiety and fears. For many years I said I didn't go to university because it was better just to get a job and go straight into work. That it was unnecessary in order to be successful and that people who went to university were kidding themselves and it was experience in life that matters. Bullshit. To this day, I hate myself for taking that approach. The truth is I was too scared to go and too scared to voice it.

The next stage of life was work. I have been fortunate to be in pretty much continuous employment since leaving school. Autistic people can struggle to find employment, so I do feel blessed and grateful for this. I have moved through a lot of jobs, but I am not sure if this is due to being autistic or being an anxious person. The feelings of wanting to be successful at my job and needing to receive praise and recognition are exactly as they were at school. However, there were new worries added to this, and retaining a job was the main one. Being in work equates to having money, which in turn equates to being independent. You now have bills to pay. Your income is essential to survival. You need money to pay the rent, run a car, buy food and clothes, pay utility bills – this list could go on. This creates one big fear for an anxious person in the workplace: what if I lose my job and can't get another? This is a fear everyone in employment might have from time to time, but I think that if you are an anxious person the thoughts and feelings about being unemployed will probably be more frequent than they are for the average person.

Being autistic makes work even more worrying for me. There is a lack of understanding about how autistic people function in the workplace. In a lot of cases, work can be an environment that is almost the complete opposite of what we need in order to be healthy and have good well-being. There are two main autistic elements that are crucial to understand. The first is social communication and interaction, the second is sensory differences.

Let's think about social aspects of autism first. Autistic people can have difficulty socializing with neurotypical people, and we live in a world where we are outnumbered by the latter. For somebody with social interaction and communication problems this can be difficult and lead to more stress and anxiety. I can find it hard at times to work with others because of it. My place of work has always been in an office, often open plan, with about four to six people. There is often a lot of office banter and small talk. There can be huge pressure on me to join in with this. Small talk is difficult for me. For a start, I don't always understand it and, when I try to be part of it, I am often misunderstood. This can then lead to anxiety.

As an autistic person, I can try and fit in by using techniques that make me appear more neurotypical to others. This is called masking and is more commonly done by women and girls, although it is not unheard of for autistic men and boys to do this too, and I have masked on many occasions.

Masking can be very harmful, especially if you are an anxious person. It can involve making uncomfortable eye contact, scripting whole conversations before they happen, researching topics that you have no interest in, mimicking the facial and physical body language of others (which are not natural for you) and doing things you really don't want to do. Masking is a whole subject on its own. It is detrimental to well-being because you are not being your true self, and can lead to a degree of self-loathing. It is also extremely exhausting to keep up with the pretence, both mentally and physically. This means that your level of anxiety will increase too. In my experience, you find yourself worrying more intensely about things because you are so tired.

An autistic person shouldn't have to mask, especially if it makes them more anxious and unwell. Better understanding is simply what is required. I also think that neurotypical people in the workplace shouldn't mask either to suit an autistic. The key thing is acceptance, respect and balance. If everyone strived for this then I am sure that it would create less anxiety for those inflicted with nervous thoughts.

Next are sensory issues within a working environment. Autistic people are prone to sensory problems. We experience sight, smell, touch, proprioception and taste at a much stronger level than most neurotypicals. This can be a good thing when it leads to sensory seeking, when an autistic person looks for and indulges in a sensory activity which is pleasurable for them or helps to calm them. Unfortunately, the flip side of this is sensory overload. When a particular sense experiences too much intense information, it can be uncomfortable to the point of creating pain for that person. Every autistic person is uniquely different and the way that sensory input affects them differs considerably. Also, an autistic person might be okay with a certain sensory event, such as a loud noise, one day but the next day it could be unbearable. This could vary depending on what other things are going on in that person's life. Sensory input can lead to increases in anxiety and stress.

This is okay in a situation where the autistic person can escape and get away from the sensory overload. However, in a working environment this is likely to be impossible. For me, strong bright lights drain the life out of me. After spending time under such lighting, I feel stressed, drained of energy and beyond my ability to function well. It can be difficult to describe this to a neurotypical person. It can seem like such a trivial thing. I know when I have tried to explain such feelings, I always think, *Oh no, I sound so melodramatic, they are not going to believe me.* It certainly requires empathy from the part of the listener. Knowing this and trying to make yourself heard can be stressful in itself.

The impact of anxiety can be huge for an autistic person. Sensory issues, social issues, environmental issues, the over-thinking and the need to mask can cause much limitation to a person's life, even during events, activities and things they might want to do.

I would describe myself as risk averse and that is due to me being a worrier. The best example I can give is the fact that as I am writing these words, my over-thinking autistic brain jumps into overdrive with every sentence I type. Am I sharing too much? What if I am saying the wrong things? What if they think what I am writing is rubbish? What if I offend somebody? Am I using the right language and words? Can people understand what I am writing? So many questions and so much stress for something that should be enjoyable...

And yet I am writing this. Despite the anxiety and the easy option of simply not writing this, I am doing it. So, the next questions are 'How am I overcoming the anxiety?' and 'What is helping me to not let anxiety completely take over my autistic life?'

## Managing anxiety with help

### Medication and therapy

As I mentioned earlier, I cannot completely remove anxiety from my life but there are many ways that I can manage it so that it does not totally overwhelm me.

The earliest management for my anxiety started with medication. After a long period of anxiety and depression as a teenager, I was prescribed anti-depressants for the first time in my life. There have since been several periods where I have been on what are broadly called psychotropic drugs, usually required after a particular prolonged stressful period in my life. The dosage has varied depending on the situation. The big question is: 'Do they work?'

Well, in my opinion, yes and no. I do not believe that medication can completely remove any anxiety. I think this because anxiety is normally caused by experiencing a problem or a perceived problem. Until the issue is addressed or solved then there is still the potential for worry. However, what medication can do, which is why I would say 'Yes, it does help', is to reduce the symptoms of anxiety. To put it simply, medication can take the edge off whatever you are feeling, and this can then allow you to face your anxiety and problems.

I now know which pills and at what dose I need in order to reduce my symptoms, take the edge off my feelings and allow me to have the space I need to work on what is causing my anxiety. This leads me on to the next aspect of helping to manage anxiety – therapy. It is worth remembering that medication and therapy often work side by side and this is the 'official' medical route to helping a person with a mental health issue like anxiety.

Therapy has been a huge part of my life and I am a big believer in it. A therapist, counsellor or psychiatrist should be there to provide a safe, private route for you to discuss your issues and to help you to tackle your problems. Often when you are suffering from anxious thoughts, it can be impossible to talk through them or share them with loved ones, family, friends or work colleagues. The chances are that the anxiety you are feeling has been caused by one of these people, which could make it impossible for you to voice what you are feeling to them. This is partly where a therapist helps, as the relationship formed between you and them is one that should be detached, so you can freely talk about your problems.

Notice I used the word 'relationship'. That is because for any therapy sessions to work, you have to establish a connection with the person offering the counselling. This is in order for you to trust them and be able to talk freely about your deepest thoughts. This does not happen immediately. It can take several sessions of therapy to build this unique partnership of detached reliability, belief and understanding with someone who is effectively a stranger to you. Once you find a counsellor who works for you though, the help can be very beneficial. I have seen the same person for many years and have found their support and advice invaluable in helping me deal with my worries and problems. It's good to talk and share.

One of the most common techniques used in therapy is cognitive behavioural therapy (CBT). This involves changing the way you think or feel about an event or situation by analysing and challenging your thoughts on the subject.

It can work and has worked for me, but it must be done in a way that suits the person, especially if, like me, they are autistic. Autistic people think differently and so the conventional ways of practising CBT might not work. Again, this is where having the correct therapist is vital as they should know how to tailor the way they teach CBT in order for the autistic person to be able to understand

and use CBT techniques. From my experience, CBT can work with an autistic but it needs to be done with the understanding that some autistic people (including me) can have very black and white thinking. Therefore, it can be difficult to persuade them to challenge their thoughts and make them see the facts for what they truly are. A counsellor with an autistic client must understand this and use different techniques in order to help that person. This could include more structured sessions, longer sessions, greater patience and even different communication methods such as visual aids.

## Senses

I am a sensory seeker and it helps me to cope with my worries. Over the years, I have identified what my senses find enjoyable and tailored them to suit my situation. For example, water is a great sensory device for me. The touch of it and the sounds it can make are really soothing, especially when it comes to making me feel better during periods of anxiety.

If I have had a really bad day, where nothing has gone right and I feel like an absolute wreck, simply having a warm bath can combat this. I use water to help me relax by indulging my touch senses, while any movement made makes sounds that are also pleasurable. It is an instant way of making myself feel a million times better. It helps to break the cycle of over-thinking and makes me feel more positive. A long soak can be a relaxing privilege for many people, but for me sometimes it can prevent and treat poor mental health, increasing my well-being.

Unfortunately, a bath does require a certain amount of time in order to work. Therefore, I have developed smaller ways to use water as a sensory aid to ease my worried mind. Simply rubbing my hands under warm water gives me the sensory sensation that is calming, and this is a really good solution because it can be done anywhere. The most stressful places that I might find myself – work, train stations, restaurants and so on – have toilet facilities that give me access to sinks. This allows me to wash my hands for a few minutes. Work is the best example – if a task, work colleague or office politics begin to get me down then I can pop to the nearest sink and run my hands under the tap to feel slightly better.

If I am really going through a bad time with my anxiety, my love of water can be taken to the next level of sensory seeking – a long walk in the rain. This combines the senses already discussed – the sound of the rain being one of the strongest sounds water can make – along with visual and olfactory stimuli. If walking in a wood, for example, the rain makes earthy smells and you can see it bouncing off the leaves of trees. However, to experience this I obviously need it to be raining at a time when I am free from other activities to enjoy it. It is especially difficult in summer or warmer months.

It is also important to realize that all autistic people are different, so it is up to the individual to discover what stimulates their senses in a good way and then tailor that as a relaxation technique. It can be anything. So, experiment – find what works for you and then build it into everyday life and use it when things get too much.

Another great technique that can help you relax is distraction. For me, distraction techniques are often a short-term fix to worries. They take your mind away from the anxiety for a while. I find that once the distraction is over, the anxiety can return. It is impossible to distract myself from it forever. I do use distraction though, as the break from the anxiety and over-thinking can give my mind and body time to reset themselves a little. It can also provide some much-needed space so that when I do return to the issues worrying me, I am better able to tackle them.

So, what do I mean by distraction? Well, it can be anything really: reading a book, watching TV, listening to the radio, playing a game. It is about engaging your brain so that your thoughts move away from the anxious ones to concentrate on whatever you are doing. The best distractions often tend to be a person's hobbies and interests. This can be anything from sports, puzzles, gardening, knitting, cooking, collecting things, and generally any activity that is interesting and pleasurable.

Autistic people often have what is called a 'special interest' or sometimes an 'intense interest', which is an activity, hobby or pastime that is both calming and joyful to engage in. When indulging in a special interest, an autistic person might become very focused to the point where they forget everything but the interest itself. This is called hyper-focusing and separates a special interest from a normal hobby. As well as forgetting the world around them, the person forgets their worries too. It is a state of blissful indulgence that is a great asset when trying to help combat your anxiety.

One of my intense interests is 'cubing', the solving of twisting puzzles such as the famous Rubik's Cube. When I am stressed, I use a twisty puzzle to help me relax. It does not matter that I have probably solved the puzzle many times, as the pleasure in using my brain to solve it can temporarily remove a lot of bad thoughts from my head. A bonus is that it is an activity I can do for a few minutes to give me some head space when I need it during the day.

## Stimming

Another thing that autistic people can do to alleviate their levels of anxiety is to 'stim'. Stimming is short for self-stimulatory behaviour and is a repeated action or activity that an autistic person will do to calm and ground themselves. Often autistic people will engage in their particular stim in order to prevent going into a 'meltdown', which is an extreme state of distress caused by many different factors.

Stims can be anything. They can include the moving of body parts (such as hand flapping), listening or watching media over and over again, engaging in the same repeated behaviour such as counting, word play, number play, to name but a few. Cubing, as mentioned above, is a stim for me and demonstrates that stimming can use objects. In recent times, fidget cubes, fidget spinners and tangle bracelets have all become popular items that people can use to help them feel calmer.

Whatever the stim, they are great at preventing anxiety from becoming overwhelming. The trick is to understand when you are becoming anxious and then use your stim to try and prevent this. You don't have to feel anxious to stim, it can be great to do just for the pleasure in it.

This brings me nicely on to the best thing I ever did to help with my anxiety – reach out to others. The old saying that 'a problem shared is a problem halved' is one that I can really get behind. However, since communication is one of the issues that autistic people can struggle with, reaching out to others for help can in itself be difficult and worrying. I feel a hundred times better when I connect to other autistic people. It makes me feel less alone, relieves my problems through sharing and makes me feel part of something.

I connect with other autistics both in real life and through social media. I am lucky to have an adult autistic support group in my area and have been attending their monthly meetings for many years.

It is a safe, open environment where problems can be discussed and analysed, and support offered. It is also fun and enjoyable, with humour, stories and special interests being shared. There is a big autism community online, which is available round the clock for those who engage in it. There are chat rooms, groups and video channels to provide advice and help with any issues you may have. Getting practical support from others can be crucial to help ease worry and stress.

## Animals

Animals provide a great resource for easing anxiety too. Whether it is a pet at home, or a larger off-site animal that you care for, they can be a great source of comfort. I am lucky enough to own three horses. I find being around them calming and just their presence is enough to relax me. I also get a lot out of looking after them. After a stressful day at work, spending a few hours mucking the stable, being in the fresh air and generally making sure the horses are fed and watered is a brilliant tonic. I don't have any house pets, but I do spend a considerable amount of time fussing the farm cat where we keep the horses. Stroking and petting an animal has been proven to increase well-being, so if you have the opportunity to do this, it can help.

## Body and mind

Finally, there are a few other ways that can help shrink anxiety and ease worrying thoughts. I like to think of these as 'body and mind' activities as they utilize the mental and physical aspects of the body. The first is simply exercise. Physical exercise can help to dispel anxious feelings. When exercising, the body releases endorphins, which are natural chemicals that when secreted into the body help us to feel less pain and reduce the negative effects of stress. This can therefore calm anxiety and give you space to deal with any problems you might have. The exercise can be anything. For me, it is going for a run, which after a busy day can make me feel much better. You could try any exercise such as yoga, dancing, swimming, team sports – whatever works for you. Try it, do some exercise, and make a note of your anxiety level before and after.

The second technique, meditation, is a practice which allows an individual to train their awareness and enter a calmer state of mind. I think of this as 'body and mind' because it focuses on both. Mentally you are focusing on your awareness, physically you are controlling your breathing. Controlled breathing is calming in itself. Taking deep breaths, counting them, holding them and releasing them is a calm, peaceful activity. It is often used in meditation practice to calm the mind, but deep breathing can be used at any time, especially at a crisis point of stress that might occur during the day. For example, if you have just been told some worrying news, try deep breathing to allow you to process it.

I have been using meditation and mindfulness, which is the state of being fully engaged with where you are and what you are doing, for many years. It takes practice and can sometimes seem as if it is making your mental state feel even more busy, but in the end it helps to create a little bit of mental space. It makes me feel refreshed, happy and even blissful. It's impossible for me to feel anxious at the same time as these feelings, and although they won't last all day, they provide a healthy break. Mediation and breathing techniques can also be used as little or often as you can fit into your day. Even a small ten-minute session once a day can be beneficial.

Combating anxiety can be difficult, and although there are lots of techniques, support, advice and tips here, they don't always work. The key thing is finding what works for you as an individual. For me it's a combination of drugs, therapy, exercise, sensory seeking, distraction, meditation, connecting with other autistic people and indulging in my interests. Experiment and find what works for you. You will then have valuable weapons to use to help you manage your anxiety and prevent it from controlling your life.

## Managing anxiety and understanding autism brings hope

I think there is a lot of hope for both autistic and non-autistic people who suffer with anxiety. The techniques for managing anxiety are the starting point for this hope, meaning that, one day, you will experience the horrible effects of anxiety less or even not at all.

Being autistic is part of me and I cannot separate it. Despite some of the difficulties it can cause, I would never want to eradicate it from me because to do so would be to destroy who I am. Anxiety exists in me as a co-morbid condition to being autistic. That I would remove without hesitation. I do wish that one day a pill could be developed that removes anxious thoughts altogether – a medication that does not change who I am, does not make me drowsy or have any other unpleasant side-effects and just simply removes anxiousness. I really hope that this happens in the future.

Until that mythical drug is produced, I will do the things I have always done to manage my anxiety and hope that it will be enough to face the obstacles that life sends my way.

One of the key aspects that has helped me to manage my anxiety is therapy. I have been lucky in my life that when I have needed the help of a counsellor one has always been available in a relatively short period of time. I have also been in a position where I can afford to pay for a private therapist when needed. I know a lot of people do not have the finances to do this, even though they need to see a qualified professional person to help them with their issues.

My hope for the years to come is that there will be more ways for people to have quicker access to therapy, whether that's through more people becoming counsellors, more therapy session time slots or other improvements to the current system. It can be a life-saver for many people, a way of improving quality of life for many more suffering from poor mental health, including those struggling with anxiety.

However, remember that any individual has the potential to help another just by listening. It might not help with all mental health issues, but for things like anxiety, just sharing worries can reduce the stress. Sharing a problem or a worry might not fix it, but it might well make the person feel less alone. The main thing is to offer to be a friend, to be there for the person and show them kindness. Show them how important they are and that they matter. It's so important to human well-being to know that somebody has got your back, that somebody has time for you. It makes both you and them feel better about themselves. In recent times, there has been more media coverage about mental health awareness, and I think people are starting to have this better understanding. I hope this continues in the future.

There are also many more resources about mental health out there than ever before. From books, websites, podcasts, biographies, forums, social media, people can share and learn about mental health issues like anxiety. This leads to better understanding and more hope that people will be able to help one another. There are even courses that people can take such as becoming a 'mental health first aider'. Legally, every company must have first aiders at work, and I hope in the future that the same requirement is in place for mental health first aiders too.

Distracting your mind from worries by indulging in hobbies or taking up a new interest might present the opportunity to contact other people and form new lines of communication. The more people can communicate, the better they can understand and accept one another. This makes me feel optimistic for a better future, where more people can get along, despite their differences. This should lead to less negativity in the societies we live in.

Hobbies and interests can lead a person to go online to interact with others. This can lead to more positive shared experiences and possibly even new friendships. The interest could be used as a distraction from anxiety, as mentioned before, but could then lead to new friends who after a while might even be a new way to help with any anxiety. They might discuss their worries with each other. This works both ways for them, so two people might be able to now help each other's mental health.

When I was first diagnosed as being autistic, I had a lot of concerns and worries about what this actually meant for my life. I had questions that needed answers. My real-life social circle is very small and had limited people with autistic experiences. It was not until I was directed to use social media that I started to encounter more autistic people. This was, as they say, a game changer.

I found people, both autistic and non-autistic, who could help me to understand myself and others better. I discovered the online autism community was varied. There were different types of people, yet some had common views and opinions. I learned a lot. Online became a place not only where I could share my special interests but also ask for advice and even give my own support to other autistic people. I hope I have achieved this when I have posted on social media.

I hope that the online autism community continues to grow and be a supportive, safe environment for many people. I hope people are kind and can voice their differences with respect. I hope shared experiences from autistic people help others to get through the problems they are having. I hope the online community continue to give some strength to those autistic people who need it. I hope that people can learn about each other, share their interests, lives or whatever they want to without upset. I hope that the online autism community continues to spread awareness to all those who encounter it.

I am hopeful that awareness and acceptance of all autistic people will continue to improve into the future. There have already been great advancements of this in human history. If you look at the story of autism in the past, you can see these changes. Just one example is the history of institutions in many countries where at one time autistic people were kept away from mainstream society. Many contained autistic individuals who with some help and understanding did not need to be there. They could have lived their life in society with the same successes and failures that everyone goes through. Now autistic people are mostly living in the community, some with more help than others, and not locked up in institutions. We can live with far more freedom than ever before.

I have only officially been diagnosed as autistic for a short period of my life. In this time, I have seen a lot of changes. There seems to be more understanding of autism awareness and more acceptance. One example is the way that some shops now have an autism hour, where they dim lights, stop playing loud music and have non-beeping checkouts. This may seem a small thing but it can mean the difference between an autistic person successfully doing their weekly grocery shop without being stressed, and potentially having a meltdown. There are more autism-friendly shows in cinemas and theatres, and more autism days at museum exhibitions, where fewer people are allowed to view the museum for a period of time. It's a start but there is still a long way to go.

The great thing is that these initiatives are being undertaken more and more. It does not matter if you take advantage of them as an autistic person, the point is that they exist. This means that somebody has listened to autistic people, autism organizations, advocates and even friends and families of those on the spectrum. They have listened and tried to do something to help. They have made an attempt to improve things.

What could be more hopeful than that for the future?

Even if they get it wrong to begin with, which with anything new is likely to happen, they have listened once and so they will listen again. The first attempts can be adapted and modified further by listening to autistic people and their advocates. Remember, it takes effort to set up an autism hour in a shop or scheme aimed at improving the lives of autistic people. The instigators want to get it right, so they need feedback from those using the schemes in order to tweak what they are doing and make them better still. That feedback can only come through listening to autistic people and everyone working together.

So, finally, I believe that having hope is important, be it for a better understanding of autism or a solution to the detrimental effects of anxiety, or anything else. Hope for me is really about the future. If the past or the present has been awful, then there is hope that the future will be better. It motivates me to carry on. We all have difficulties in life, mine is anxiety and I manage that. I am also autistic, which does have a few negative aspects but also a lot of positives. I am hopeful that these negatives will become fewer in the future as more people understand, accept and respect autism.

Life is tough at times. It does hurt. There is help though, and there is hope. It's a great journey.

# Hoyo (Mum) and Inankeedii's (Son) Journey from Hurt to Hope with Autism

NURA AABE

My name is Nura, I am British-Somali and a mum to an autistic boy, Zak. Zak was diagnosed when he was three years old. I remember being told he had autism, but I did not understand. There is no word for 'autism' in Somali. The only equivalent word in my community's language is similar to 'mental illness'. Devastation hit me. How could my son, my beautiful boy, be mentally ill? I loved Zak dearly, but I felt that it was the end of the world. Anxiety and fear overtook me in the beginning. Questions about my son's future rolled around in my head: What happens to Zak when something happens to me? Will he ever be accepted for who he is? Will he ever speak? Will he ever be independent? Will we ever be accepted in our community? Zak was my first child in an arranged marriage, as is the norm in my community. I had my own expectations, expectations from my husband, and expectations from my community about what being a mother meant. I was suddenly thrown into a role that was nothing like I had expected.

I remember sitting in meetings with professionals and not understanding what they were saying because they didn't accommodate for the fact that 'autism' was new to me or that I was from a community that doesn't have any language for what was going on. For a long time, I had panic attacks out of fear for my baby. I felt hopeless and alone. Not even my husband understood. At night, Zak wouldn't sleep, so I remember having to sit downstairs with him to allow the rest of my family to sleep. I would sit there wondering if I had done something wrong. I would ask, does he not love me?

Zak had a lot of challenging behaviour. He could be very aggressive, particularly as he grew. He would bite and kick, he would destroy toys, rip up his clothes, spit in the food I would cook. I always had, and still have, a constant alarm bell in my head. I look back now and realize how much it affected my mental health, but at the time I just wanted to hear my son's voice. Between his fourth and seventh years, I remember very little; I think the sleep deprivation and constant fear meant I didn't form any memories.

Zak and I had to also face the Somali community. In Somalia, there is no understanding of difference. Any difference like autism is seen as mental illness. The people who are 'mentally ill' are lesser in value, or not true citizens. Where the UK was in its attitudes towards autism a hundred years ago is where Somalia is now. Having Zak meant that my credibility was in danger. Before Zak I felt confident in my community, but that disappeared when he was born because I felt that my community would not understand or accept me and Zak. Members of the community would say things without understanding the negative impact they would have. I had even to teach my own family about Zak. I felt stuck between two identities, stuck between two very different theories of autism. I was torn between Western and Somali ways of life and thinking. But at the same time, I didn't fit in either. I don't know how to describe how it felt to lose that connection to my community.

Zak was about six when I read an article about autism, and from that I decided to attend a conference about challenging behaviour in people with autism. I dragged my friend along with me because I was so nervous. I didn't know what to expect. By the end of the day, however, I felt so much relief. It wasn't just me going through this struggle with their child. The fears I had were similar to the fears other mothers had about their children with autism. In hindsight, I think that day changed my and Zak's life. I reached a point where I realized that I could either accept Zak for who he was and do everything in my power to support him, or carry on struggling and hold on to my previous expectations about what and who Zak should be. I chose to accept Zak. I also chose to be proactive, to learn what I could, and to challenge the system.

To begin with it was a steep learning curve, it was like trying to learn a whole new language. Zak went to a special needs school, but after a while it was hurting me to see him get out of the car and go into that building. I knew Zak deserved better; it was not the right educational provision for him. I took him out and home-schooled him. We went through phases of trying different approaches, some were very strict and rigid, others were more flexible. I tried everything I could to help my boy. I read everything I could to understand my boy. I learned that he was trying to communicate he was in pain or distress when he was being aggressive or destructive. Learning this meant I could start to understand him and help him feel comfortable. Of course, I felt guilty that I didn't realize he was in pain or hurting before. But we were finally getting somewhere. I learned to take the tags out of his clothes, and he stopped ripping his clothes up. I learned that he needed a sensory diet to help him cope. I learned how to give him information in short and concise ways. I learned how to show him where we were going before we went, so he could understand. I learned so much. I started to feel as if there was hope for Zak and me. I have become good at problem solving in order to understand what Zak needs. He was trying to communicate through challenging behaviour, and when he was understood, the challenging behaviour was not necessary.

My biggest worry for Zak was whether he could ever be independent. I wanted my boy to be able to live his life and be happy. Part of being independent is being able to communicate. Zak didn't speak for a long time, but some of the interventions we tried at home helped him to reach a point where he could use language. I will never forget the day he said 'mam' for the first time. It was beautiful. He even started to learn to write.

When Zak reached puberty, things got a little difficult again, and it was too hard to home-school him. But as Zak was much more able to communicate, he went back to school after nearly ten years of home-schooling. This time he didn't go to a mainstream special needs school, he went to a Steiner school. This was a turning point for Zak. He loves nature, animals, outdoors and being active. He started working with a young man, to whom he really connected, in this school. He started to go climbing and to the gym, and he would go to the supermarket. He was starting to flourish.

I also went back to studying. I went because I wanted to learn more about autism in order to help my son. I did my undergraduate and master's degrees. I had learned so much about the system, about myself and about autism. I had spent years challenging the system. Having to fight for my son's social care and education. Having to fight my son's corner in tribunals. When I finally accepted

Zak for who he is, I got the courage to fight for his right to have the care and education he deserved. I had to fight the system to give Zak the opportunity to flourish. Sometimes I had to put myself at risk, both in my Somali community and in my British community. But I know what is right for my son, I know intuitively what my son needs, and I had to make sure I was listened to. I don't think professionals realized how much I love my son, or that my love for Zak gave me strength to challenge the system.

For a long time, I think people forgot that Zak was a person underneath the autism. People saw the label rather than Zak, particularly in my community. But I am challenging that now too. I want me and my son to be part of our Somali community. I want my community to accept us for who we are. I have set up an organization to help other families in a similar situation to me and Zak, to support them, but also to challenge and change the way my community views difference.

I feel empowered to keep going. I feel empowered by my son. I have started my doctorate to help the autism community within the Somali community and beyond. I will be Dr Aabe – something I never even dreamt could happen. The journey I have been through with Zak has changed who I am. Zak opened my eyes to the world.

Zak is now the most joyful young man. He is fit, tall and sporty, he loves climbing and riding his bike. He is also very handsome and cheeky. I watch him and can see how much he wants to learn. Zak is a very brave young man. He is loving and caring, he tells me without words how much he loves me; he comes and kisses me on the head (he is much taller than I am!). He is proud of me. He feels happy and safe. He is so happy. It is beautiful to see him so happy.

The future can be a bit frightening for me and Zak, it can bring uncertainty. Our future is working out how to be happy from this moment to the next. As we go, we try to build days, months and years free from anxiety. We embrace what we are doing and who we are. We never shy away from autism and what has happened to us. I have so many questions for the future but seeing Zak happy and healthy gives me hope.

# Big Brain Trees and Superpowers

## A Journey of Discovery, Patience and Understanding

EMMA COBB

## Hurt

I live, breathe and sleep autism. I have three children, all on the spectrum. I am a clinical psychologist working in an autism diagnostic team. And I am autistic. There is a trend these days to 'tell your story'. I, like many, feel I have a story to tell. In the last five years, I have been thrown into the sea of learning about this superpower my family possesses. Part of this learning involves reflection over the decades of my life when I did not know why I was different. I am constantly experiencing 'aha' moments. Something pops into my memory from my childhood and there is a sudden 'aha' as I finally understand what was going on back then. Now I can explain it alongside the underlying template of autism that I never knew was there. I can find myself starting to react in a situation that others seem to be managing, and 'aha', I realize what is going on to unsettle me – it is the bright light, the subtle background noise, the mismatched patterned carpet or the slightly wonky picture that is throwing me into chaos. Knowledge has brought understanding and with it a difference in my acceptance of myself.

In my work, when our opinion is that the life experiences an individual describes fit with a diagnosis of autism, we talk to them about John Fisher's Transition Curve.[52] This model was initially put forward within the work environment to consider how employees deal with change. For us, the model applies to any change within a person's life. Receiving a diagnosis of autism has had a significant impact on my understanding of myself and the life I have so far lived. The process of assessment and diagnosis ticked many of the stages on Fisher's curve – anxiety about receiving a diagnosis (if I wasn't autistic, then what the hell was wrong with me?), happiness (relief at finding out that I was not making it all up), fear (how is this knowledge going to change things? How on earth do I explain this to people?), and anger at the fact that no one ever picked up on it and cut me a little bit of slack. Anger with myself for being an idiot. Guilt for being an idiot. It continued. It still does, and I believe that the emotions Fisher describes do not follow a straight line. I will often have a lightbulb moment remembering something from the past and realizing 'that was autism'. I catch myself doing something now and recognize it is my Aspie self making a stand. I believe that this will continue throughout my life now.

I never really realized that I have been anxious my whole life. Well, that's not entirely true. I knew I was anxious. I never realized that this level of constant anxiety was not experienced by everyone else. Everyday things – speaking to other people, going out of the house, making a phone call, making a choice – required so much rehearsal, so much scripting, and created so much anxiety. I did not realize that my anxiety was not normal. I believed that I was different because I was particularly bad at managing that anxiety. Even though I scripted in advance every possible conversation and scenario, I still couldn't get a handle on the immense anxiety. What was wrong with me? So with that came a sense of being inadequate, overwhelming low self-esteem, and a lack of confidence to be able to do everyday things that everyone else did with such ease. I believed that I was somehow flawed.

Every experience I had confirmed these beliefs about myself. I was – and still am – constantly misreading situations and other people. I am never sure if what I said or did was the right thing to say and do. As a teenager, I was particularly bad at the boy/girl thing. I would miss the signs of being flirted with and I would see those signs when they were not there. I ended up making a complete fool of myself on so many occasions. I would go out of my way to place myself in the awareness of someone I was interested in; I would overbearingly try to force someone to be my friend. I scared people and they backed away from me. I suffered so much agony around trying to get it right and always getting it wrong. When I look back on my teenage years and early adulthood, I see a time of deep hurt and depression. I was constantly questioning why I always felt so lonely. I remember sitting in my room sobbing as I pictured a future of forever loneliness. Would I ever be able to form friendships and relationships that didn't feel awkward or exhausting? I threw myself into dangerous situations and connections with people that were not healthy for me. These tended to reinforce my sense of low self-esteem and confidence. Trying to get your sense of self validated through social interactions that are poisonous is a rocky road. As each one confirmed I was not good enough, I sought another one to try to change that belief. So, the downward cycle was perpetuated.

Throughout life I have always worried about what others think of me. I have no confidence to make a decision, to do something different, to wear something new. As a teenager, I merged into the fashions of my friends and would copy the styles of those I aspired to. If a friend bought a particular set of earrings, I would follow suit. Even now I will buy something slightly different and it will hang in the wardrobe untouched. On occasion, I will put it on, only to remove it quite quickly in fear of what others may think about it. If on the very rare occasion I do go out of the house in something that is slightly different, I am on edge. If I hear someone laugh, I assume they are laughing at me. My busy brain is constantly analysing if the rest of the world approves of my decision. One of the worst questions my husband can ask me is what I would like for dinner. Not only am I making a decision for myself, I am also trying to decide what other people will be eating. What if I get it wrong and choose something they do not actually want to eat?

When my son was eight, he explained to me that one of the differences between people with autism and those without autism is that 'autistic people have bigger brain trees with lots more branches'. He is absolutely right. He is also very, very wise. Our brains do not have a setting that says 'that's enough thinking'. We go down every single branch possible, twice if needed, and do not stop until every possibility is covered. As my son so rightly points out, the autistic brain is very busy. So ask me to make a choice or decision and my mind will be occupied well into the night. Every thought process will have an underlying current of anxiety.

I think my first major crash came alongside a major life event. I had finally met a soulmate who was able to understand me. It hadn't been easy getting the relationship right and I made some mistakes, but he stuck with me. We had bought our first house, got engaged, and were holidaying in Scotland when he was killed in an accident. My world shattered. I can't tell you how it felt or how I got through because I don't really know. Autism and grieving can be quite a strange experience. We can be painfully logical about death. I had learned all about the grieving process through my training, so I became my own research project, testing the bereavement theories. I became furious that I was over-analysing the experience and not just getting on with grieving. A friend who had lost her partner in the same accident was, in my eyes, doing it so well. In comparison, I couldn't even seem to get grief right.

A friend told me that I was particularly 'weird' at this time. I now think that for a few months I stopped masking my autism because I just couldn't do it. It no longer mattered that I pretend to be normal to make everyone else feel better. I think people saw the real me briefly – the meltdowns, the difficulties with being around people, the need to isolate, becoming absorbed in hobbies, switching off socially because I had reached my limit, and drinking to make being with people easier, becoming extroverted and uncontained. Yet I could finally do this with a valid excuse that the world accepted – I was grieving. People have a sense that grieving is a difficult thing to do. The world does not have a sense that camouflaging autism is hard work. But if you do it well, they will never know.

It's important to say that at this point I did not know I was autistic. I was 29 when he died. I was 48 when I was diagnosed. When I think about the hurt that I have experienced, some of that is feeling bereft that so many people I loved will never know and never be able to finally understand who I was. So much could be explained if we had known. I want to go back and say that I am sorry. I wonder what my parents would have thought about the diagnosis. After reading my assessment report my sister recognized similarities in herself and has also since been assessed and diagnosed. We have a lot of conversations about what it is to be 'Aspie and proud'. We can see that our father had traits. Would my parents have understood and felt that a final piece of the jigsaw puzzle was put in place? I am not sure they really understood what it was to have a grandson with autism – the only one in our family diagnosed during their lifetime. Autism has a stigma attached to it fuelled by media portrayals of the extreme and rare cases. We are emerging from a generation who found such things shameful. I often encounter people who are terrified of receiving a diagnosis and being given a 'label' that there is something officially wrong with them. I do not see autism as something lacking in myself. I feel neurotypical with an added dimension, maybe the next step in evolution as we progress away from time-wasting small talk and start to use more of our brains.

When I look back, I see that my life has been very complex and confusing. If I had known I was autistic, I may have been able to make sense of a lot of that. I don't think I would have experienced any less anxiety or any less complexity. After all, the world is a confusing place. I do not like people. They are unpredictable and expect so much from me but never say what those expectations are. How can I get it right when no one tells me the rules? What would have been different is my perception of myself. I would have been less self-critical, kinder to myself, less questioning about what was wrong with me. I would have understood my identity better and not needed to throw myself into the wrong situations to try to work out who I was.

I suffer with something that many autistic people know far too well – what was once described to me by a service user as 'resting bitch face' (RBF). I would be so rich if I had a pound for every time someone said to me, 'Cheer up, love, it may never happen.' I am happy, okay? I always have said that my natural face is expression-less. I now understand that this is part of an autistic characteristic – other people do not know how I am feeling because my facial expression may not match my emotional state. This means I can hide how I am feeling, and it avoids people asking me awkward questions. Talking to people is awkward enough. But the downside of RBF is that, alongside the frustration of constantly having to explain that I am not upset and that I do not need to 'cheer up', on many occasions I have felt at the edge of despair and no one has noticed. So let's add that to the emotional mix – decades of believing that people did not care about me, that my emotions were pointless, meaningless and unjustified. My inner thoughts often criticize me for assuming what I am going through has any weight in the world. I live in a world where I do not think my emotions and opinions are worth anything. Consequently, I keep quiet and berate myself afterwards for not speaking up. I worry about making a decision or putting forward a point of view. If I do speak out, I over-analyse and question – did I do and say the right thing? In my own head, I can never win no matter what direction I take. My brain operates with a curtain therapy approach – 'pull yourself together'. After all, the rest of the world seems to be able to manage this life thing. Get over it and fit in.

Being a parent of autistic children comes with a whole heap of social awkwardness. My children do not fit the expectations of parents with neurotypical children. It doesn't take long before the party invites dry up, the little cliques of parents shuffle you out onto the side lines, and you become excluded. Invites to grown-up get-togethers dry up. People who would have once given you time to talk in the playground begin to look towards their disapproving clique if they get caught up in a conversation with you.

Conversations become quick and uncomfortable. Whereas before I could mask my way through a decent chat and keep a conversation going, I am not given that opportunity to pretend to be normal. There is nothing more soul destroying than seeing those photos on Facebook of an event you were not invited to when in the past you would have been. Social situations are difficult, but it doesn't mean I don't want to give them a go. I would like to have the choice, not to be ostracized for who I am and who my children are.

I feel that my family have been the victims of what I can only describe as 'witch hunts', for example opportunities offered to my children that are mysteriously withdrawn at the last minute, or my children being asked to leave groups when their autistic behaviour is uncomfortable to other parents. I can't help but think that when certain parents get wind that my child may be part of a social gathering they threaten to remove their children. Perhaps paranoia is also a side-effect of autism.

I have hurt. I do hurt. My mental health has taken a battering as I exist in a world that expects me to be more like them and less like me. I cannot let go of the mistakes I have made, or the injustices others have done to me, and each one brings a barrage of emotions that are overpowering and never dwindle. A strong sense of social injustice is a very common thing with us autistic people. It does help to look back and realize that I wasn't a weird or broken person, I am an autistic person trying to fit into a world that isn't quite my shape.

## Help

My first experience of formal therapy was after my partner died. It was all very nice to sit and chat to someone. I am really good at talking about myself, and I have had a rather colourful life that people like to hear about. That can fill a one-hour therapy slot quite nicely. But most of my experiences of therapy did not really help me that much. For starters, I am a therapist who is also autistic, so my logical mind argued that I should be able to fix myself. If I couldn't do that then I wasn't all that good at my job. But therapy also relies a lot on an exploration of emotions. Autistic people are not particularly good at recognizing their own emotions. One of the most difficult questions is often 'How are you?' and we are lucky to have 'Alright' as an option. Alright covers the range between 'Barely functioning' to 'So happy I could float'. It's a good cover-all. I know that outside my working role when I ask someone how they are, I probably am not all that interested in knowing. If someone were to actually tell me how they were, I would probably cringe inwardly. And if they burst into tears – oh help! Offer a tissue, a cup of tea, a gentle pat on the back – 'there there'? I do the socially acceptable thing. I am lucky, I can go into my clinical psychologist script and I have an internal manual of what to do. It is very learned, so once we get beyond the equivalent of an hour's worth of therapeutic intervention I begin to flounder. I have run out of verbal response options and I am exhausted by playing the role.

Therapists have a skill of being able to sit in silence and wait for you to fill the gap. When I am in therapy it has involved me not being able to truly describe what is going on no matter how much scripting I have done in advance. I end up saying what I think the therapist wants to hear – that I am alright and getting better. Because of my mismatched facial expression, I also give off the body language that I am totally fine. I am discharged quite quickly as being 'fixed'. I then return to a sense of feeling that my emotions are not justified. Even the therapist thinks I am okay. I feel like a waster of other people's time. So not only am I terrible at managing my anxiety compared to the rest of the world, I am unjustified to even think I should seek help. Considering that fear of being judged, as I embark on another journey down that brain tree, there is a strong desire to not actually want to try that therapy thing again because of what others, including the therapist, may think of me.

I have seen four therapists in my life. The first and the last ones both told me the problems they have had in life, leaving me feeling that I have nothing to worry about in comparison, further invalidating my belief that I need support. Perhaps therapy is not always the answer. Having said that, one approach did help me. It was a very visual approach and very clearly defined. Social interactions were described in a very clear way to me so that I could attach roles to those people within the interaction and understand what was going on, almost in terms of a script. I was able to make sense of where things had gone wrong or how they needed to be managed in the future. Despite not knowing I was autistic, transactional analysis was a therapy that helped me to understand the complexities of people without realizing it was something I did not naturally understand.

If therapy is going to work, it has to be right for the person. The therapist needs to understand autism and, at a very basic level, start off with working on some shared understanding of what emotions are before even getting to the 'How do you feel?' part of the session. If therapy starts with an expectation that the individual will be able to express what the problem is (and let's face it, why shouldn't that be a reasonable expectation in a neurotypical world?), then those involved will encounter a large barrier. It is impossible to be able to explain a complex emotion and the triggers to this if that emotion is not recognized in the individual. A lot of people I have worked with will say that they know all the words for the emotions, but they do not recognize these as being applicable to them. Why have a dictionary of words to express happy, angry and sad when these three words are enough?

So what does help me? First and foremost, I recognize that I get over-peopled, and when this happens, if I do not take time out on my own, my head feels like a pressure cooker. There is a physical buzzing that feels as if it is going to burst out of the top of my head. This I now know is the 'pre-meltdown phase'. If I keep going, I will pop. This will sometimes be an explosion of anger but more often it is a shutdown. I will walk away from any conversation, I will go mute, I will hide. That is not a very useful strategy when you have a family and a full-time job. Therefore, I need to ensure that I never get to that point. Understanding the idea of social energy[53] has helped me enormously in that it gives me permission to do the things I need to do to 'unpeople' and restore my energy levels. I have levels of helpful strategies depending on what life will allow me. If I have the time, I do photography. I go out in the world to places away from people and I take photos. I capture things that look right to me. I lose myself in the Suffolk countryside, absorbing myself in what I can see and how that can become a picture. I belong to a photography group and do occasional shoots to learn more skills. They are usually three hours, by which time the group situation has challenged me, and I get quieter and less sociable as the shoot progresses, watching the clock to see if it is nearly over. If I cannot get away from home, as is often the case, we have a building in the garden, 'The Shack', that has exercise equipment and a DVD player. As often as I can I go down there to exercise and lose myself in a box set. I have spent many an hour accompanying Frodo on his travels, hoping Jack Bauer will be okay, and learning the story of

*How I Met Your Mother.* If I haven't been able to get to the shack for a few days I can feel it. I feel the pressure cooker ramp up a notch and the buzzing in my head starts.

I have hobbies. Granted, they can change like the weather and what once absorbed me for hours is cast aside. I currently crochet and create orders for other people. In the past I have done cross-stitch, diamond painting, dot-to-dot books designed for adults with 1000 dots (numbers make me very happy), musical instruments, mindful colouring, to name a few. Notice that all of these are solitary and absorbing interests. There are no people involved.

In the last few years, I have joined a choir. I love singing. I love dancing. There is something predictable about music and it satisfies my soul. There is a bit of a contradiction here. After all, the choir is big. It's full of people. I have made friendships (I will come back to this one in a minute). I love the singing. I get the harmonies. I am good at it. I pick up the part and often others rely on me to take the lead. The hardest bit about choir is the break. All that small talk. On one occasion our choir leader told us that during the break we had to find someone we hadn't yet talked to and get a conversation started. I went into panic. An autistic person's nightmare. A friend who knows I am autistic took me by the hand and led me round, breaking the ice in every conversation, and taking the social lead. Without her I would probably have excused myself to the toilet for half an hour. In a normal week when we aren't being forced to 'mingle' I follow the same routine – same drink, same place to sit, look at phone. People do know that sometimes I need to be on my own during the break. That helps. Honesty about what I need also helps. Having my diagnosis has enabled me to identify my needs and understand the signs that I am overwhelmed.

Friendships. This is a weird one. A group of us from choir have connected and we do this thing where we go to each other's houses for a meal, we look after each other, we do those things that I am told friends do. It's a very weird concept to me. I can't really ever remember having a good solid friend; I have always been part of a group, feeling a little bit on the edge and as if I am there because others may have felt sorry for me but not really feeling like I belong. The one group I have been a part of for a long time is a group who barely ever see each other. When we do meet, it may be for a whole weekend, which I find really difficult as it is a full 48 hours of masking. Whenever we meet up I am praying that I can have a room on my own so I can be alone. These friends probably don't believe I am autistic because I have strategies to cover up the bits that I find really hard. This new group of friends, from choir, are people who live in the same area. We see each other regularly. It feels very odd and my brain often tells me they are just being nice having me along – I still don't get it – but they know I am autistic and they look after that part of me. We meet little and often. I am learning how to be part of this group and they do know it is something I have to work on. A work in progress. I still wish I had one good close friend, a 'bestie'. I am not sure I know what it is to have a best friend. That is actually about realizing and accepting that what I am experiencing is a friendship. I can doubt my interpretation of these relationships and talk myself out of the idea that they mean anything to the other person. If I hit a major crisis and had to turn to one person in my life, I don't know who that would be. I don't have a text buddy. I have lots of good friends, but I still feel alone.

After my diagnosis, I began to write a few 'words of wisdom' of things that I have learned about myself, and it seems right to share those here:

1. Understand your autism. Be able to understand that some things are about your brain's wiring and you just need to think about them differently. It is not because you are useless or stupid. It's just that life teaches us to operate from one book, *The Book of Neurotypical*, and autism likes to use a different manual on occasion.

2. Understand yourself and acknowledge the superpower that you possess. You do not lack something that other people have. You have everything that they have plus you have something extra. You can be whatever you want to be, but if you do not understand yourself the natural hurdles will feel insurmountable.

3. Social events are hard work. They exhaust and overwhelm you. It is okay to take yourself away. Go to the toilet, sit down, cover your ears and close your eyes. Rock if you need to. Switch off the environment for a few minutes.

4. People are confusing. I often come out of a situation wondering, 'What happened then?' I don't know if it went well, if I messed up. There are things I just didn't get. Learn to be kind to yourself. Feeling befuggled isn't your fault. I repeat – people are confusing.

5. If it feels comfortable, explain your autism to people. You are the expert on you. Ask them to give you more time. Explain that you process things differently. Tell them when you are having time out from people. Get an ally who can run through things they have observed within social interactions so that you can talk it through with them. That way you don't have to spend the next few weeks reliving and analysing everything that was

said and done. When you can't read people, knowing if you got it right is impossible.

6.  Change. People leaving my life feels wrong. I find it really hard to let go of people and will stay in touch with people who actually have no meaning to me. I don't like the change in my life. Learn to understand the way life cycles. People move on and it is not about anyone, it's just about life.

7.  Patterns are distracting. It's impossible to concentrate when the pattern of the carpet is out of sync. Teach yourself to break away from staring at that carpet. It feels uncomfortable because that out-of-sync pattern does not go away, but you can do it.

8.  Numbers. They calm me, distract me, they are reliable. I often lose my concentration of the matter at hand as I start to calculate how many men versus women there are in the room, what age groups, percentages, how many are younger/older than me, how many times that colour is repeated in that stupid carpet. You name it, I can analyse it. Before you know it, I've missed half an hour of discussion and they are asking me a question. Dammit. I subjected myself to a football match recently. Couldn't tell you who our team were playing or who won, but I can tell you that the away team had 283 supporters in the stands, which was less than 2 per cent of the total crowd.

9.  Understand that some things just feel wrong. I remember as a teenager they refurbished our local Woolworths, made it bright and white and full of fluorescent lighting. Going in there made me feel physically sick. Back then I didn't know why but it is a very strong memory that it was really wrong in there. Tapping,

background noise of a crowd, some materials, they just feel wrong. The reaction is physical and there are no words.

10. Life does turn us into pressure cookers. An underlying bubbling tension, a buzz of discomfort, a knowledge that at any point things will shift across to 'not coping' mode. How that comes out can be unpredictable – tears, mutism, anger, fear, running away, fury, actions through our hands or feet, words, or becoming nothing. Only then does the pressure cooker cease. It is possible to let off steam regularly before the pressure builds. Control the things you can control in your environment – control your time spent there, give yourself moments to be away from people, use ear plugs and dark glasses, control the lighting and so on – to minimize the impact on the pressure cooker of what you cannot control.

11. You can be flexible with how you do things. Shopping – all those people, music, things around you frequently not in the right place. I often come out without the things I went in for. Processing the act of shopping with all that sensory overload is exhausting. Pick your time to go. I put a list on my phone and delete things as I go along. And that list is well organized into the different sections of the supermarket. Trolleys can be very grounding. Lean into one with your body and feel the pull of the earth. No one will bat an eyelid if you stand in the shop staring at your phone to try to control the busy environment. Ask if the shop has an autism hour. If they don't, suggest one. Self-service checkouts are the best thing ever invented and apparently in some supermarkets you can mute that irritating voice as well!

## Hope

I would like to think that I have hope for the future. I am seeing a changing society where autism is becoming more talked about. We have autism hours in supermarkets and autism-friendly screenings at cinemas. The phrase 'reasonable adjustments' is becoming more used in everyday language. Sunflower lanyards[54] are a blessing in our household. I don't always wear mine, but if I need to go out and I am feeling the pressure cooker is building up, I will wear it.

Sadly, I have also sat in conferences where professionals and leading names have talked in a very 'them and us' way, stirring anger inside me, as I sit in a room being talked about as if I am not there, as if I am some unseen minority. A particularly renowned speaker stood in front of a conference proclaiming that autism was caused by brain injury at birth and that these poor unfortunate souls need to be allowed to be part of gardening projects in head injury establishments. I was quick to clarify her facts for her and I probably got a larger round of applause than she did as the audience seethed at her words. At those moments, when I hear influential people perpetuating the idea of a less heard minority, I lose hope.

But there are people out there who have passion for change and are fighting for a better world. There are books that tell us of successful, if not difficult, journeys through the neurotypical minefield. More and more people that the world respects are discovered to be autistic. And these people are speaking out about their experiences. There are famous names 'coming out' as autistic. Uncomfortable as it is to hear, I have been told that I am 'inspirational' (I don't receive compliments very well) – I have a family, a full-time job, a doctorate no less – and I am a slap in the face to the stigma that autism is a disabling and hopeless condition. Tuck me away in a gardening project at your own risk.

At my darkest times, I must have found hope from somewhere. Animals have always been incredibly important to me, and the knowledge that I am important to them keeps me functioning. Being needed gives me hope. At these times, I am more to the world than just a dysfunctional Aspie. Producing something for others gives me a sense of purpose. When I receive a photo of a child holding on to a crocheted toy that I have made I feel I have achieved something. I made someone smile. I keep a diary and try to write down my achievements for the day in it. When I feel I am slipping, I can look back on these and see that I do have worth and value. I hope for change, and that whatever I do I am contributing to that.

I often have long conversations with myself about talking about my autism. At work, people can be very open with service users if they have dyslexia, colour blindness, a slipped disc. However, depression, anxiety and autism are 'hush-hushed' and to talk about experiencing them is overstepping boundaries. I am quite comfortable telling people I am autistic, but only if it is the right thing to do. I am not a militant Aspie. I don't shout it from the rooftops. But I don't hide it either. To do so perpetuates the myth that it is something to be ashamed of. Openness and honesty are key to building a hopeful future. I have a big investment in the future for people with autism – after all, that's where my children are headed. I fear for their teenage years as teenagers can be ruthless and will stamp on other people's vulnerabilities. My hope is that learning about difference and sameness is embraced in the early years; that it is not even thought about as it is the norm; that as our autistic children grow into adulthood the world accommodates them without a second thought; and that reasonable adjustments are made without a long-winded analysis of why and what. Every business should think about every individual's needs regardless of any hidden diagnosis. One of the first questions should be 'What can we do to help get the best from you?' and there should be no shame to give an honest answer, be it ear defenders or permission to not have to sit in the staffroom for lunch.

It is corny to say it, but every change does come from within. Until we feel comfortable in who we are and happy to voice our needs, the rest of society will feel uncomfortable. If we cannot say what we need then nothing will change. Learn to be comfortable with yourself. I remember proudly telling a doctor that my son was autistic and him looking at me with sympathy and saying 'I'm sorry'. There is much learning to be done, and those of us who have the knowledge and experience of what it is to be us and what we need are the foundation for future change.

Hope is important. Without hope we have no cause. I hope for a future where we are all equal, where we do not have to fit into one mould. I would like to think that the media redefines what is 'normal' and that it is not one size or shape anymore. It is only society that defines neurotypical as the norm. It is society that creates an environment that does not match the needs of the neurodiverse. Because we cannot fit into this predefined expec-tation we are thus defined as not normal. Let us do away with these rigid and socially driven templates of normal. I would like to see friendship groups filled with a mix of all neurotypes, all levels of mental wellness, and nobody having to pretend to be like everyone else to fit in. It is not much to ask to just allow people to be themselves without judgement.

# My Journey to a Place of Hope

## Autism and Schizophrenia

YENN PURKIS

I am an autistic person who also has a diagnosis of atypical schizophrenia. I have had my autism diagnosis since 1994 and my schizophrenia one since 1995. I have taken medication for over 25 years and have had several episodes of psychosis and mood issues in that time. I am an autism advocate and author and I also work almost full time in the Australian Public Service.

My early life was hellish, with bullying all through school. I got involved in drugs and crime as a young adult and found myself in some very dark places, including prison and some fairly brutal mental health forensic facilities. I have overcome a very troubled life and some poor choices to become an accomplished and satisfied person now. I am something of an anomaly. That being said, my mental illness is a constant and frightening companion. I am susceptible to mood issues, and every time I get anxious for a prolonged period I am on high alert as this often leads to the onset of psychosis. While outwardly I may seem very successful, there is often a battle going on within and I never take anything for granted, knowing I can become unwell so easily.

## Into hurt

In September 2019, I got my kitchen renovated. Maintenance of the home I owned was always a stressful matter for me. Knowing that this kind of prolonged stress could be a trigger for psychosis only added to my anxiety. I was determined to be okay about the kitchen, but circumstances conspired to make life very difficult, with the new kitchen becoming a catalyst for one of the worst episodes of mental illness that I have had. The plumber working on the kitchen renovation had needed to order a special sink as the kitchen bench was a non-standard size. The joiners got all the cupboards and bench tops installed but the sink had still not arrived. The company doing the renovations sent me a photo and all I could focus on was that the taps were still there over a solid bench top with no sink. I was terrified that the taps would somehow turn on in my absence and flood my apartment. On top of this I was going through extreme stress at work for a number of reasons and my psychiatrist had very recently prescribed me medication for ADHD – which was essentially amphetamines. Psychosis loves amphetamines and my experience was no exception. Within days I was in a scary, dystopian, Alice in Wonderland nightmare, and reality was something which happened to other people! I ended up in a psychiatric hospital for five days and then went to stay with a friend as my kitchen was not yet finished and being at home caused me unbearable stress.

While staying with the friend I had some highly stress-inducing work phone calls which catapulted me from the state of being quite unwell to that of being acutely psychotic. I saw dead bodies in my friend's car, I saw ghosts in the mirror and thought the world was ending. My friend took me to my psychiatrist who sent me to hospital again. This time I stayed for six weeks. I don't really remember the first three weeks in hospital. My main recollection was that I had loads of visitors, some of whom I knew and others who followed me on social media and whom I had never met in person. I felt totally overwhelmed by the onslaught of visitors and their doubtlessly thoughtful if perplexing gifts. I even asked the nurses to tell people not to visit me as it was all too much.

I was in a very dark place. I was psychotic and more depressed than I had ever been. I was also quite prone to anger. I remember doing some fairly full-on 'advocacy' for a fellow patient whose parents were being ableist and rude to him. I went into his room and yelled at the parents, telling them, among other things, that they should care about their child and support him rather than blaming him for his illness. I also had a major meltdown in relation to a troubling email. I was so depressed that I didn't care what happened to me. This was a dangerous situation. I had a lot of suicidal thinking and planning. I was in the grips of Hell and I could see no escape. My home was an ongoing source of extreme anxiety and going home on overnight leave from hospital was very challenging indeed. I thought that I would have been happier sleeping under a bridge than in the home which I owned with all its maintenance issues and the ensuing stress and misery.

I gradually improved but progress was not a linear trajectory. Just before my discharge date I became toxic on one of my medications. I was taken off this medication the same day I was discharged. I could see that this was potentially going to cause issues. I asked the hospital doctor if I could be put on a different mood stabilizer and he said no and that my private psychiatrist could manage my meds outside hospital. I left the hospital with a great sense of concern about going home, particularly going home without the medication which had so suddenly been stopped.

Home was as horrific as I had expected it would be. Every interaction with the plumbing caused extreme stress. Flushing the toilet, turning on the kitchen taps, filling the kitchen sink, using the washing machine, using the shower – all of these were an ordeal and resulted in a spike of high anxiety. I worried about using the plumbing even when I wasn't actually using it. I worried that my new kitchen would break – that the splashback would come away from the wall or the cupboards would stop closing properly. Being at home was a perfect storm of stress and misery. Within three days I was also feeling the effects of no longer being on my mood stabilizer medication. I went back to work on the Monday, which was also stressful. On the Tuesday I took the bus home and on the way started to worry that my shower might be leaking. The stress I was having at work combined with anxiety about my apartment put me into a place where I felt totally helpless and defeated. I no longer wanted to live.

I saw no future in the world that had given me so much pain and drama. From my worries about home, to my anxiety at work, to the hospital doctor taking me off my meds, to the terror I felt about the supernatural, God and Hell, my life had become unliveable. On the way home from work I went to the pharmacy and collected some medication with the sole intention of taking it and dying. I was an advocate, an autistic role model, but I didn't care. I was a friend, sibling and child and I didn't care. I had a responsible job, several published books and a home and I didn't care. I lost all sense of connection to the world. I don't even think I gave up, I just stopped feeling part of things. It no longer mattered. This was a sort of liberation, albeit a very negative and dangerous one. I didn't care about what all my followers on social media might think or my friends and family. It was not a conscious or intentional disconnection; I was simply no longer connected. I decided that suicide was a strategy, in fact it was the most effective strategy of them all, the ultimate solution to the chaos that had become my life.

I took the pills. I sat in my living room for a couple of hours, feeling in control for the first time that I could remember. I felt calm. I had done it. Eventually I felt conflicted and called the mental health crisis team. They sent an ambulance and I hated myself. I found myself alone in the emergency room crying uncontrollably. And I was alone. I was too ashamed to call a friend, so I spent the night with nurses being thankfully kind and supportive but with no friend for company. The only things that prompted me to call a friend were that my beautiful black cat Mr Kitty needed to be fed and my phone charger was at home and my phone was about to die – unlike me, who was apparently as incompetent at ending my life as I was at living it. Once I told one friend it made it easier to call another. I ended up telling three friends and my mum about what I had done. I was full of blame and self-loathing. I was in the medical ward for three days. I was hearing the voices of everyone in the ward insulting me and saying horrible things. I didn't know if these were real voices or not, but whichever way it was terrifying and confusing. I got out of bed and pleaded with a doctor who was writing his notes to make it all stop – the voices, the sadness, the pain.

Hospital is often no place for an autistic person and this was definitely true for me. I was subjected to constant noise and light and nurses poking and prodding me. From the medical ward, I was sent to the mental health unit, the locked ward and one of my least favourite places in the world. My problem with the unit – or most of my problem at least – was that there is a huge power imbalance between staff and patients. The staff spend their time in a glass 'fishbowl' behind a locked door. If you knock on the door, they will open it, if you are really lucky. They will often just ignore you. A lot of the staff there treat patients with disrespect. It is not a nice place. Usually when I am there, I am in the midst of psychosis so am mostly unaware of what is going on, but this time I was well enough to be painfully aware of the power imbalance.

Anyone who has read my autobiography will know that I spent five years in the 1990s as a prisoner. This was a very traumatic time for me and I have struggled with post-traumatic stress as a result of my time in prison. During this admission, the unit reminded me very strongly of prison. I was triggered and in all manner of pain and torment when I was there. Essentially, I *was* a prisoner. I was on a court treatment order so couldn't leave the unit. I became angry and overwhelmed. For the first time in almost 20 years I started self-harming. One of the staff even said 'schizophrenics don't self-harm' as if either my experience or my diagnosis was not true. In fact, I was self-harming for the same reason I had while I was a prisoner. To my mind, I had no other options and it was a means of taking control for myself in an environment where I had none. I was actually worried while at the unit that I would commit some petty criminal act and end up in jail. I was taken to the high-dependency unit a few times and spent time in the de-escalation room (previously known as the seclusion room). I was trapped and saw no hope for escape.

## Finding help

A saviour unexpectedly arrived while I was in the depths of misery.

One of the doctors at the unit thought I would benefit from a residential mental health service called Step Up Step Down.[55] I had used this service many years previously and found it helpful. When the doctor suggested I go to Step Up Step Down I was delighted, although I didn't believe it would be possible for me to go there given how angry and self-destructive I had been at the unit. It was 23 December and I was resigned to the idea that I would be staying in hospital for Christmas. A nurse told me I had a visitor. It was the manager of Step Up Step Down, Manon. She spoke kindly and she clearly understood what I was going through. I thought she would refuse my application due to my recent self-destructive behaviour but instead she told me I could join the programme. I asked when this might happen, expecting her to say in two weeks' time, but she said 'tomorrow'. I was saved! Knowing I was going to a genuinely therapeutic place made the next 24 hours manageable. I felt less disempowered and had some hope.

The programme was lovely – staff were kind and supportive and the residents were friendly. I felt as if I had travelled from Hell to Heaven, all due to Manon understanding that my behaviour at the unit was caused by me being triggered and traumatized rather than being poor behaviour on my part.

I spent Christmas Day at Step Up Step Down. My contribution to the lunch was a strawberry cheesecake which I made from scratch. My parents were invited by the programme staff to have Christmas lunch at the house. It was a lovely day and about as different as Christmas in the unit as you can imagine! I felt as if I had been saved by Manon and the wonderful programme she ran.

While I was at Step Up Step Down I participated in group activities and learned some helpful strategies. One of the best things I learned was the idea that if you have an anxiety-provoking thought it was best to imagine that the thought was a person knocking on your door. You could choose to let them in or not – the choice over what to do with these thoughts was entirely up to you. I adapted this thinking strategy to imagining the problem thoughts were Donald Trump knocking at the door. When an anxious or catastrophizing thought arrived I would just think *Eek! Trump's at the door* and figuratively not let him in. It worked wonders.

I also formed relationships with the other participants. Sometimes this was a negative thing as my autistic hyper-empathy meant I worried about people who were having a tough time, but mostly it was a lovely thing to connect. One participant was almost certainly autistic and we got along really well. When I am unwell I find those connections with others having similar challenges really positive, affirming and supportive.

The next few months were still challenging but things changed and often changed for the better. Recovery is not a linear journey, and I found myself in hospital a few more times. My most recent hospital admission was at the rehabilitation hospital at the University of Canberra. This facility was unlike anything I had encountered and was genuinely useful. I learned strategies and gained hope during my time at the university hospital.

At the university hospital I had access to a multidisciplinary team comprising a psychiatrist, peer workers, a psychologist, occupational therapist, social worker, allied health assistant, dietitian, exercise physiologist, art therapist, key worker and nurses. These workers had regular meetings to discuss each patient's progress. I was at the hospital for four months. The psychiatrist was constantly telling me that there was no pressure on beds and I could stay there as long as I needed to. Of course, I didn't believe this for the duration of my stay but the psychiatrist was actually correct and, unlike most of my previous hospital stays, my discharge date happened when I was genuinely ready to go home. I was put on a new medication when I was at the university hospital and this made a big difference. Medication is different for each person who takes it, so I will not recommend one or other medication here, but it is nice to find one which is effective.

The time I had at the university hospital was very helpful. One of the key factors was that the staff were caring and respectful. This had not been the case at the mental health unit, where staff attitudes were patchy at best. When I was at the university hospital, I started on a graduated return to work. This was actively encouraged by my treating team. I would stick a note on the door of my room saying I was working until 1pm (or whatever) and just get on with it. The staff even brought me an ergonomic chair from their office so I didn't injure my back from working at the desk in my room.

One of the more significant drivers of my recovery was my own attitude. Even when I arrived at the university hospital and was very unwell, I had a positive attitude. My motto was that I was there to get better and that I, not my illness, was in charge of my life. That attitude made it a lot easier to ask for and access help. In contrast to my time at the unit, I saw the workers at the university hospital as being on my side. This made it a lot easier to access assistance. I benefited from seeing a psychologist at the university hospital. We worked on a module based on the dialectical behaviour therapy model called Distress Tolerance, which was all about accepting that hard times will happen and working through them rather than trying to avoid them at all costs. I left the university hospital as I had never left hospital before – ready to go home and actually feeling good. I am forever grateful to the staff there.

## Towards a place of hope

It is now over a year since I became unwell and needed to access a lot of support from hospitals, community programmes and rehabilitation services.

I firmly believe that life is a matter of meeting the challenges we are presented with and learning strategies to make our respective worlds easier to navigate. Difficult circumstances can either defeat a person or be used as the basis for building self-knowledge and resilience. My most recent episode of illness has taught me a lot of approaches which will help my life to be less difficult in the future. I have learned about radical acceptance and 'sitting with' difficult times and learning from them.

I am not always positive and I do not always have hope but I have learned a lot about managing my illness. Each episode of illness in my life has taught me something different, from self-knowledge and insight to wisdom and acceptance. Viewed in this way, my illness is not entirely negative. In fact, an episode of illness, seen with the benefit of hindsight, can teach me a lot of useful attributes and qualities. While it is very unpleasant to be unwell it can also be seen as a chance to learn and grow. Another positive element related to my being unwell is the connection I make with fellow consumers as well as mental health workers and clinicians. I have some long-term friendships forged during periods of mental illness and hospital stays – people I was in hospital with or simply fellow travellers on the difficult road that is life with a mental illness.

For these reasons, I do not hate my illness. Sometimes I wish I didn't have it, but I do have it and it is not possible to wish it away. So if I have to have an illness, viewing it in terms of the positives as well as the negatives is the most hopeful and helpful approach.

I do have hope for the future. However, that is not hope for a future free from my schizophrenia. I have had schizophrenia since 1995 and I have taken medication for it since then. It is not going away. It is part of my life and I need to accept its ongoing presence and influence. Hope is not about wishing away my illness. Hope is more about being aware of my challenges and limitations and working to learn skills and strategies to manage it and share these with others.

I give a lot of presentations, mostly about autism. I gave a presentation on autism and mental health to the staff at the University of Canberra hospital a couple of months after I was discharged. This was a lovely thing to do. My topic was autism and mental health and the staff were very receptive and had some great questions.

I used to say that if I could bottle my insight and resilience and give some to everyone who is autistic and has a mental illness then I would willingly do so. If I learn something it makes me happy to share it with others so that they can have the benefit of it as well. I hope that my work on mental health and autism will change the world just a little bit, that my experiences will help others who are autistic and have mental health issues to live fulfilled lives where they are respected, heard and understood. I hope that my work will help mental health workers to better understand autism and to treat their autistic clients with respect and understanding. I can see these changes beginning to happen, which fills me with hope and encouragement. This sense of hope is an essential part of my life and my work. Hope drives what I do both as an advocate and as a human. We all need hope.

# A Particle of My Existence

CASEY CHONILY

## Hurt

Mental health starts with an autistic girl adapting to a world that does not adapt back.

Walking up the mountain of despair, I felt wobbly and hurt inside. In hindsight, the hurt was like a grey darkness, the texture of a broken television screen. I do not know why at aged four or six I felt like that. But I did, and it was the start of my mental illness. Even at three, I remember at night tracing the shadows of traffic and feeling that first grey hair of depression.

I find it hard to explain how I feel about the hurt I've experienced, and my head hurts trying to explain it, in the way it does when I am surrounded by too many people or have done too much in a day.

My experience of hurt creates a darkness over my eyes which I cannot change. The world around me almost reflects that darkness, which can make me very pessimistic about the world. Even when I am somewhat okay, it reminds me of this dark narrative that exists, the perspectives born in mental illness that I cannot get away from. It's like an annoying adult checking up on me when I was a kid.

For a while I was not aware of my challenges. It is still challenging to understand these problems, let alone articulate them. I found it painful how when I communicated to the psychiatric staff, and crisis team, I was not understood. They thought they understood me, which was at the very least annoying and at the worst led to misdiagnosis and unnecessary injections.

Most neurotypicals are not good at understanding or assessing the needs of people with autism. This is a great detriment to many people, including the family and other people in a neurodiverse person's life, as they must watch these people get ignored and even mistreated. So, as an autistic person there is pressure to do your own research in a way you probably would not if you had a physical health condition. I tried to become aware of my mental health, autism and learning differences. I obsessively researched them and now I am maybe too aware. I can no longer turn off from worrying about difficulties, as I could when I was ignorant of my challenges.

The articles and books I read, when trying to understand myself, provided a great source of discovery and comfort. When I relaxed, I was able to connect to the material a lot more and see myself in it. The clarity they provided about the depression I experienced was hugely useful; I had been very insecure over whether or not I had depression. My dad had said that I seemed to be depressed a couple of times, but the memory of the nurse who spat that I was not depressed when I was sectioned still gnaws in my throat. But the information I read in the articles and books legitimized that it was depression.

I recognize the symptoms of my depression now: the tired heaviness, as though wearing steel-capped boots, how you mask in public, how every movement is exhausting, and how a grey cloud of anxiety clogs your throat. I can wake up at different times each day: Monday 1pm, Saturday 3am and so on. This disconnect from society's circadian rhythms increases the isolating aspect of depression. Although, when I am awake at night it feels like a part of me can breathe, and there is a safety in fewer people being awake. Admittedly, for a part of my life I would traipse through the night like a translucent fox, my freedom was no people. I do not do that now; I am terrified of going outside during the day, let alone at night.

I know that I very often outwardly do not seem ill enough. But internally I match people's autobiographical descriptions of mental illness or autism, and the articles on depression and other mental illnesses. I should get help and support. I know my wounds are generally deeper than people are aware of from my vocal expression. When I express myself through writing, people suddenly believe differently, such as my support worker who said they 'had no idea' and 'it's very truthful' after reading some of my writing. I am surprised by the truthful comment because my wounds are deeper than I even express in my writing.

I struggle to understand sensations in my body, and my emotions. This is referred to as alexithymia and is common in people with autism. It can be a very frustrating, non-painful brain freeze. Panic attacks thread from a small gasp to violent dizzying chokes. Agoraphobia and social anxiety are similar. The panic attacks taste like sweat, I see the discolouration of the sky, and experience a mixture of fear and anger at anyone who comes near me.

I have to mask, and having mental health issues has increased the masking. The masking feels like going into a type of shock, where I cannot be me as I can when I am on my own. I cannot see myself anymore. I feel myself slightly on the outskirts. I can feel my mouth moving around with words and my eyes playing along.

Depression is a sigh that never quite leaves my lips. It is blue, with sterilized black. Sometimes depression is painful, seeping into small holes in my joints.

Most things stop me pursuing life. I am aware of how much agoraphobia affects me and it may be useful to discuss this more closely. Around nine years ago, I had my first panic attack. I was due to hand in geography homework that I had not done. When the geography teacher mentioned that I might have had a panic attack, I scoffed, for reasons I do not understand now. I guess in the past I was not very understanding of mental illness in general, let alone believing it would engulf me. Now it is embedded in me.

The panic attacks progressed to agoraphobia, which is linked to the non-treatment of panic attack disorder. Agoraphobia crept in with a sluggish routine, which slowly built up into my daily habits. I stayed in while depressed, to the point that going outside was fearsome. I spent a year at my nan's but I was afraid of even being near her and her drill-sergeant routine, so my bed became where I lived all day. For the past seven years, when I have lived alone, I have mostly been depressed and anxious, and these ingredients have meant that my bed was my safety and my comfort. Furthermore, being in a psychiatric ward for a while with all those people, I barely crept out of my room due to social anxiety, let alone outside into the fresh air of the garden, which felt like false freedom.

In the first psychiatric ward I was sharing a room with five other people. For the first week, I mostly stayed in my room, or should I say 'section'. I did not know what was happening to me, I was unbearably angry. I was too afraid to be around people, and so I pleaded to eat in my 'room'. This was met with irritation, until I cried. Why do I need to cry to be listened to? At night, they would use a torch that flashed a painful brightness into my eyes. I tried to communicate that I felt I had autism. Psychiatrists stared at me blankly, as though I was both a riddle and an idiot. In the end, they ignored me and misdiagnosed me with borderline personality disorder. I was grumpy and irritable and was deemed difficult – *clearly due to my autism!*

I get why I was grumpy, but I did not have the level of awareness then or use of language to communicate. People such as psychiatric staff who did not know me would twist my words and reality into something strange to me. I was only 21 at the time and took their analysis seriously. I was trying to shape myself into someone I was not, so that I could understand what was going on.

I think the psychiatric ward hurt me the most when it came to agoraphobia. I was too afraid even to leave my bedroom there. It was a small room, and while staff knocked on the door, they would then just barge in before I could respond (which caused shutdowns with the odd meltdown). Even my room was not private, and this made me quite unwell.

My version of autism is a need for a space to build up energy again, after the exhaustion caused by people (even if I like them). After a while, I feel a jarringly dull-pitted claustrophobia being around people, such as I felt in the psychiatric facility. I survived by turning my needs off, sadly.

In the psychiatric ward, if I left my room I would be with 50 people on a varied spectrum of unwell and irritable patients to falsely joyous staff. The best option was to stay mostly on my blue, plastic bed and slowly read or, now and again, watch a DVD (there was no wifi so this was a treat). It was sterilized boredom, where you are controlled patronizingly with a dose of pills spread throughout the day, and unhealthy food (so many potatoes!). I did not join the smokers, a habit many take up due to boredom, because it was too social for me. Television involved sharing the remote and being around people. When the living room was empty, I felt a calm turquoise breeze in my throat. But then someone would come and sit without saying anything, and then stand and leave, or stay in silence, or say hello. This was all unnerving and I would feel pressure to change the channel or leave myself.

There was never any space just to get your energy back from the exhaustion of being around people. It was almost like trauma; I could not regenerate, and exhaustion layered over more exhausted flesh.

They stated on their notes that I was fine; I felt their anger that I was taking up a bed. But this treatment of dismissiveness was painful; I was so close to a breakdown, except I was not comfortable enough to have it, so it got embedded in my tissues and cells.

I had the same experience later, in similar supported accommodation, except they were not allowed in your space (but they did have keys to get in). I barely left the flat except to set appointments and when the cars were gone. Living for a long time with this invasion of privacy and the already not dealt with panic attacks led to agoraphobia. I cannot believe the 16-year-old who left the house at 6am to walk two miles to get the bus for her animal care course. I marvel at the many things I used to do, which now feel impossible.

However, where I live now is in a rough area with drug dealers, domestic abuse, noise that hurts me and burns me in anger, and a dodgy landlord. But it is the noisy, gossiping neighbours that irk me the most and make me timid to leave and be seen by their judging eyes. Then there is the very busy road, as loud as a stand-up comedian. But it is my only way of leaving. It is a sensory kaleidoscope of dog shit, cars and of course PEOPLE. I forget the beauty of the clouds and birds swirling rhythmically above my head. I just feel trauma.

When I try to communicate my mental distress, people do not listen, as it is not their version of distress I am expressing. I communicate with fewer facial expressions, hand gestures and body language than a neurotypical might emit when, for example, saying 'I'm suicidal'. In the first psychiatric assessment interviews (before they decide to help you or not), I thought I was like Robert De Niro with my subtle facial expressions (I had not even thought about the body language!). But instead, perhaps, I was overly sensitive to body language and conveyed the message that I could handle myself. And perhaps neurotypicals need louder, less sensitive communication.

So maybe all those people who say I am tone deaf to humans because I have autism should wonder why I can understand and connect with many fellow autistic people. We are different, not defective. Being told I was defective, whether due to having mental health issues or autism, is what has hurt the most psychologically. They see me as neurotic, a liar, manipulative, because I say heavy things without the subtext of body language and tone of voice. It is the trauma of being held by the throat by the ignorant. The ignorance of some neurotypicals is dangerous.

## Help

Mental illness has helped me. It breaks away the disconnection between people who are considered outcasts and me. I have experienced mental illness alongside learning differences, autism and physical issues. Having these challenges has made me more empathetic and less afraid of others who are different. I no longer feel a barrier between myself and someone who has a facial tic or cancer, for example. I also see not only what challenges them, but also the other elements of them. That does not mean to say I am not cautious. But I have lived the experience of an outcast and see this experience in others and no longer shy away from them. I am forever changed because of the things I have gone through and it has made me more empathetic to others. They are, generally, strong, interesting, compassionate and worth talking to. It would be my loss if I did not say 'hi'.

Also, learning about my challenges helped me understand them and manage them. In particular, knowing they are real has helped me see that I am not deliberately being a 'lazy, defective loser'. I have a different brain, which needs different strategies to survive in a world not designed for me. However, there are perks to having a different brain, such as being incredibly interested in something. This gives a speedy, joyous high that is the antithesis of depression.

Mental illness changes your thinking. The purple blue bruise of low self-worth can be survived. Trust me, you will crawl out of your pain. Look how you're helping yourself right now by reading this book. It is helpful to know that in the future, when you experience another challenge, you will SURVIVE IT!

One day you are going to realize that your thinking is not progressive enough, you do not have enough understanding of trans people's rights, black people or gay people and so on. You may have some negative discharge about your own gender, or mental health you experience, the shame of who you are. This is where you show that bruise of low self-worth and challenge your own thinking. Do not be afraid of that, depression was partly right, we are wrong sometimes. So, feel that ignorance, but instead of feeling bad, learn from it, cognitively change. There is no shame in being wrong; you do not necessarily have to be right. But listen to other voices besides your own. Own the bruised feeling.

It's important to realize that there are many minorities and 'outcasts' who are made to feel that bruise every day. Therefore, our own bruises allow us to be more empathetic towards others' pain. This helps you be a better, kinder person.

I have many things I would like to say about 'help', and many things I would like to share. In the spirit of being concise I will add subheadings and keep my explanations to short paragraphs.

## Finding my version of mental illness

I feel my obsessiveness in psychology and autism was to understand myself and communicate with people who were not listening, such as friends and family, nurses, psychiatrists and support workers. Being misunderstood leads to burnout and being unwell. However, often my pursuit of getting people to understand me pushes me into burnout because it is a lot of work. In the past, I tried to fit myself into whatever psychiatric staff wanted to see.

More specifically, filling my head with pathology made me worse. So, I took a break and tried to avoid fitting myself into disinfected versions of mental illness from scientific books and articles. I found my own version of mental illness, which was a gift – a gift because I allowed myself to listen to me.

Now, when I do read something, like an article or research paper, I can relate to it more as there is less pressure to fit the concepts discussed. The material is also less in charge now. I sometimes question the material: Is this really my version of mental illness? Is the writer someone who has no sense of being different or of the trauma of how it feels to be different?

Try not to create a version of yourself from books, articles and others. Be you.

## Socializing

I look forward to the groups I go to. I may sit on my own or with people with similar challenges. It is a safe place to chat and do an activity, even though I mask how I feel, and they seem to think I am someone very different. However, I may hear some different perspectives on mental health, which breaks the ice that has been steadily forming in my head, while at home in isolation.

The ASD group allows you to see a mirror of yourself and feel connected to a part of your identity much diluted elsewhere. Also, it is a break from judgement, so I don't worry about saying the wrong thing. The people are not demanding, just honest. I hear language used in a way that is soothing and inclusive. *I get these people! I like these people!*

Going to the ASD group makes me realize how often I am bullied unknowingly by people. They do not realize when they laugh at me or ignore my presence in the room that they make me feel lesser.

I also went to a group with a mental health charity for a while. It allowed me to be less isolated and talk about my mental health issues with others in a more honest and knowing way. The charity, most of all, has provided me with a safe place. They ran some courses which, in hindsight, weren't particularly meaningful; however, completing one caused me to feel less inferior academically. A depressed, anxious person re-learning that they could achieve something means more confidence to go back into education, socialize and even consider work.

## Writing

I joined a mental health writing club, which allowed me to find a healthier vice than self-harm, or food and television. I found myself writing my feelings down; my fingertips burnt in speed as I wrote on my laptop screen. By the second semester, I improved and had meshed several works together. They were put into the annual booklet for the writing group. I worked hard on them and the topics involved autism, discrimination, childhood challenges, self-harm, depression, anxiety, and mum issues. I was wary of putting myself out there – that awful arachnid fever of being judged. But the manager gave me some of the nicest compliments I have ever had, for anything. I showed my auntie the writing, and she said I could be a writer.

Now I know it is possible that they were just being nice. But that did not seem to matter as much...as I had still put myself out there. I would never have done that before; a curdled grey fog would have got in my way. Now I am writing this essay and I have entered a poem for a competition.

Writing is the only way I am comfortable communicating, expressing something that is important to me. I find it helps people listen to me more when I write down how I am feeling, rather than when I verbalize it. When I speak, people just do not hear me.

Writing also provides me with a healthy buzz, as does the rearranging and developing aspects of a piece. This provides my brain with an exhaustion, which replicates meditation. It is good for my mental health. I also appreciate it as a medium to express research, fiction and factual writing about my own life. This gives me numerous perspectives about myself and the world, providing more nuance and a thickened grey matter.

## Holly and animals

Animals are stereotyped for being an Aspie's blanket comforter, and for good reason. Holly was a small Jack Russell, with white fur and a mostly black face. She was beautiful, if not slightly chubby. I was lucky that she was a desperate dog, desperate for affection any time. I was able to have just the right pressure of her weight on my tummy and thighs for many hours daily. I stroked her back, face and, sometimes, wet snout. I was elated when if I paused from constant stroking she would knock my arm with her nose and make a noise as if to say, 'Ow, stroke me.' The importance of that touch, for a low, lonely teenager, was infinite. I had a creature I felt safe and comfortable to connect with, to trust.

Depression caused her to get fewer walks from me. She has sadly died, as you may have guessed. I hope one day to have a dog as magical and kind as her. But for now, I still trust a random cat or dog crossing my path for a stroke. Animals provide people with autism with a safe bridge to intimacy and contact that is not overwhelming. Also, they don't demand more than I can offer.

For people vulnerable to manipulation and exhaustion from neurotypicals' overly complicated way of communication, a dog, or even a slightly less doting cat, provides a break from that. For you and that animal, you are mutually hit with pure love!

## University

Many of us feel a bit dim. You are not dim. But you must go on your own journey to find that out. I am still on that journey of self-belief, and, dare I say it, confidence. Doing an online university access course helped me enjoy learning in a way that was not as pressurized as a degree. I also noticed that my hobby of research and reading over the years meant I had enjoyed learning for a very long time. I had attempted university before and it was where I had been at my most unwell, which made me lose my confidence. The access course helped me see I was capable of a higher education. I awkwardly treasure the words from the examiner saying I had a special voice, and that I was 'clearly very capable and intelligent'. I find it hard to gulp down compliments. To me they're like shards of glass spiking into my internal organs. But this compliment made me believe I could go to university.

At present I do my degree part time, as that is what I can manage. I can say I just about cope and I am in my second year. It is not easy, but that is not what this is about. Doing a degree is one of the hardest things I have ever done. If it is possible and I'm fortunate enough to have help (ASD specialist, study skills specialist, course tutor), I'm going to keep going.

Also – and I feel cocky saying this – despite all my failures, I have this belief now that I am smart. I feel so brazen saying that and I would not say it in a room full of PhDs. But for some reason I think underneath all the self-hate, neuroses and mental illness that I am worth something. I am. I mean, I must be in a really good mood to believe that.

The online university degree aids me in moving forward academically. This could lead to me getting a job I enjoy and becoming self-sufficient, which is very important to me. I will have a choice over my own life! There is nothing better than being independent, deciding how to live your life and having the ability to give back to the community. To have something to offer yourself and others.

One discomfort is that I am getting more support in education now than I did in primary and secondary school and college put together. I find it morally wrong that most people with challenges have to claw their way into higher education. Support and diagnosis should happen before many of us give up hope on academia. The mistakes teachers made in my education created huge stains, which cannot be removed. However, it is a great relief to be finally helped with university.

## I suck my thumb!

I come home, my shoulders compressed into heated steel edges, my aura a painful haze scattered with midges. I walk upstairs to my bed, slightly swaying, but I will not faint. I always make it. Comfort is sought. I land on my bed. Grab a blanket and stroke it. My thumb simultaneously goes in my mouth. I suck, sometimes until there are bite marks on my little thumb. My heart rate loosens its grip on my throat. I am safe. I am safe.

This has been an important survival technique since I was a child. It has possibly stopped me abusing drugs, or myself, or even others, as it allows me to find my pulse. Others think it is so sad, so defective. 'Bless her', 'Ugh, gross with her childlike habit', while they do more 'adult' behaviours. Coffee scents their breath with a smell that makes my nostrils flare. They use adult 'crutches' to help them survive: coffee, alcohol, drugs; they are in denial. While I lie, waiting for the panting to stop, not addicted to anything 'adult'. I am safe.

## Interests

I try to spend time on whatever interests me. When I'm feeling down, I find something that interests me, and it helps. It helps regulate my mood, especially at night when my medication makes me feel depressed, anxious and restless. Poisonous dread builds up through the day, for the night. But my interests help me feel better. I experience a flooding, or even love, for things. That is my version of the best happiness ever.

## Organizing the day/week

I have a notebook to organize my day. It has an 'Appointments' section, where I put things like 'Seeing support worker, 3pm – she's always late so try to cope with that'. The notebook has a 'Things to do' section and a 'Notes/sketches' section. In 'Notes', I split it into sections for medications, food, getting dressed, teeth, bath, blow dry, hair and makeup, with boxes for ticks for each. I get the glorifying satisfaction of ticking a box and staying focused. This helps me to be more motivated after bouts of depression where even the smallest tasks are exhausting.

There are also three subsections under 'Notes': good parts of day (I studied, I saw my brothers), good aspects of body (I have nice eyes, my brain remembered a lot today), and bad parts of day (very anxious, didn't study, neighbours noisy).

I really struggle to remember all the different medications I have to take. One solution is a repeated alarm, several times a day. Also, my support worker got me some blister packs, where the chemist organizes the medication, so I make fewer mistakes, which helps as many tablets are small and white. A further tip with medication is that if you are clumsy like me and lose pills when popping them out of the package, put them into a bowl first and then retrieve them from there.

After a while, the groups I go to, or putting the bins out to be collected, for example, become ingrained in my routine. Some things are a bit more of a challenge depending on my mood, such as cleaning the house, or myself. I would recommend washing daily or every other day. Do not worry if that seems exhausting – it is about creating habits, which takes time. Maybe the first step is getting into the habit of brushing your teeth. Get an electric toothbrush to do the movements for you, like I did! The toothbrush can have a timer, so you do not even have to think about timing the torture of cleaning your teeth, it is done for you.

On bad days, I try to stick to my routine. This can help me come out of a bad mood, which can be a pleasant surprise. Admittedly, I can still have TV days but not to the extent as before when I didn't have a routine and all I did was watch television. I also try to have things in the house to help me cope with daily activities, such as ear defenders for noise, mp3 player for when I'm outside, speakers to feel euphoria, food, a dark quiet room, and thumb sucking! I am now making a care box to use for immediate comfort and stabilization.

## Advice on food

I eat food when I am sad. When I have this hole inside me. And then that hole gets bigger when I lose control and eat!

But remember, food deserves to be a part of your body, health and enjoyment. You deserve to exist. Your size does not mean you are a failure!

# Hope

## Defining hope

Hope feels alien to me, like happiness. Not necessarily because I do not feel it, but rather because I do not understand it.

As a teenager, I never thought of happy or sad. As an adult, having a nervous breakdown meant I never contemplated happiness or sadness, or melancholy or joy. That is, until my brain became cruel, like shards of glass ferreting into my skin.

I still do not completely recognize these emotions, although I am better at grasping parts of my identity, mood and thoughts, but not to the extent that you can ask me what hope is, or how it relates to me. What the sneakers is hope?

I could be difficult and say hope is escapism from your life in the present, and a coping mechanism for when things are terrible. But what about when this is just your life? It hurts my brain to understand it, hope that is, I feel a fool. It is a relative of joy, right?

So, I look at joy and ask – what the icicle-inducing headache is hope?

What is hope? Because I do not know.

## Being different

Neurodiversity provides the benefit of thinking differently, and an understanding of this being a good thing brings me hope. Different is not always seen as something positive, despite it being the place of anything innovative. Furthermore, my differences, my neurodiversity, such as autism and ADHD, are not just challenges but strengths. With ADHD you can be the creative ideas person, an entrepreneur, or just the person who thinks of something interesting to do at the weekend. People with ADHD and autism have an ability to be hyper-focused, which can provide them with enjoyment, make them good researchers or even specialists in a certain field. Seeing myself as having those possibilities/strengths and many others helps me believe I can have a more interesting and special life. On a human level, being different makes it more likely that you will try to not make anyone feel the way you have felt, because of your differences. It is in my consciousness to try my best to help other people, and to have more self-worth.

## I hope for the future...

If I had to choose my biggest hopes for change, they would be for the climate change issue to be sorted out, animals not to be abused, politicians and people in power to be less manipulative, people from all different backgrounds to be given fair opportunities, and people of all different shapes, sizes and backgrounds to be allowed and accepted. These issues filter heavily into my consciousness and subconscious every day. Positive news, climate scientists, Greta Thunberg and other people making changes in this world give me hope.

I hope to be working as a journalist or using one of my interests in a museum, like English, animals, the environment, learning, autism, mental health or archaeology. I hope for myself and my family to be safe, especially my mum. I hope to improve my friendship skills and date with confidence, and to be less isolated. I hope to be more okay with me, as I think that is the only place I can start to improve from anyway. And then I would hope to work specifically on being more outgoing and trying new things. Also, I'd like to be outdoorsy and use my bus pass to go anywhere, not be trapped in the routine of staying in (remember that agoraphobia thing I mentioned earlier). I hope to reduce the fear of being in this world, and furthermore, be more cultured, open minded and mature.

Just a shallow one – I hope to not age outwardly. This is probably due to pressures to be female and having body dysmorphic disorder, a condition that makes the person find it harder to age. I hope to appreciate my body for more than its skin and contours. I hope to grow appreciation for my brain for all it does rather than focus on what it does not. I hope to feel that heartbeat of happiness, instead of the Bugs Bunny thump of anxiety.

I have hope for myself because I have changed for the better in certain aspects of my life, so it stands to reason this can continue. Life may feel like a big anguished slug, but in the trying you see there are positive amazements along the way.

## Hopeful about pills

I take antipsychotics (to prevent psychosis from the ADHD pills) that make me depressed, anxious, and restless at night. The ADHD pills cause nausea. I still take them all, as I hope the ADHD pills can make me concentrate for university, read quicker and listen better in social situations. I hope I stop getting all these side-effects or not be as bothered by them.

## Hope for autistic people

I have more hope for autistic people for many reasons. There is more support and awareness for girls with autism. This I have seen personally, in books written by and exploring issues for females with autism. More females are also realizing they are autistic (often changing their perception of themselves and life) and being diagnosed.

There is more discussion about the different strengths in autism, rather than just the 'abnormalities' and 'defects'. Also, there is debate about the extent to which autism is a disability, and 'normal' (neurotypical) people not meeting us halfway. As well, there are more places for people with autism to communicate and educate others, in research, blogs, books, YouTube, Facebook.

There are more autism researchers and specialists who are themselves autistic. This means our way of seeing the world and functioning in it is more fairly and accurately depicted. I feel the storyline about people with autism, created by the manipulative, mostly male scientists, psychiatrists, psychologists and 'pseudoists', is being shredded. No longer can they get away with telling the nodding society that I am damaged.

I remind myself that autism has a journey and to not be so angry at mistakes of the past, if these were well intentioned. One autistic researcher, Dr Damian Milton, came up with the double empathy problem.[56] This theory expresses how people who have different perspectives will struggle to understand each other. Two neurotypicals will communicate as easily as two neurodiverse individuals do. But a non-autistic person and an autistic person will find it harder to communicate with each other, as they communicate differently, their perception is different. Essentially, an autistic person's communication skills are not problematic, it is just that autistic people are outnumbered. Also, it is easy for a person with autism to feel that their perception of the world is defective as there are fewer autistic people to communicate with. Dr Milton's theory made me angry for a while, as it made me aware of how faulty I had been made to feel. But now this theory is a deflector when people start treating me ignorantly or cruelly, like a second-class citizen. It gives me hope.

I remind myself that I have much-needed variation. We have contributed so much, considering that we must spend huge parts of our lives adapting to other people's demands, while our needs often barely get met. It is amazing that anyone different, from skin colour, physical disability, mental disability, learning disability, sexuality, gender challenges and so on, gets somewhere in this world. But we do, we support and fight for each other! And I am determined to find a niche in work and socializing. That is what this double empathy problem theory communicates to me. There is a place for us. This makes me feel courageous and hopeful.

Lastly, autistic people themselves give me hope for demanding more from society. Through education, more autistic people can understand themselves better. They are realizing they are not defective, but different. Thank you to all the people who fight for the rights of anyone different, as together this leads to a better and fairer world.

## Therapy

I am aware that I need therapy. But the adult information is often too complicated due to my autism. I find it hard to understand emotions and feelings. I also struggle to concentrate on therapy due to the ADHD and it is hard to grasp the meaning of the language used due to being dyslexic. I have found a healthy workbook. I have also purchased therapy workbooks more appropriate for kids and teenagers. They are more visual and clearer in their language. The migraine of just trying to grasp the language is reduced, so I can get through more of the workbooks on my own or with others. This opportunity to understand and work through my emotions gives me hope, as it may improve my well-being and help me manage my mental health. And most importantly, it may make me feel safe!

## What now?

For me, to feel I can keep going is to have hope. I am trying to find solutions to my challenges and work through them to the end, growing a bit stronger and wiser. I am a fixer, a solution hunter. I will find ways to help my eyes glisten slightly with hope, and keep myself safe.

# Thriving Through Words

## Finding Your Niche in a Neurotypical World

JESS/JAI WHITE

My identity has been an ongoing point of constraint, bringing me both pain and joy. I was adopted at a young age, and although my adoptive parents were very open with me, I was always one step ahead, constantly looking for the answers to questions that hadn't yet been asked. I was lucky enough to find a family that was 'passable' as my own. Growing up mixed race always brought its challenges, as did adolescence, but combine the two and my undiagnosed autism and the word 'complex' does not suffice. At school I was very much the outsider; too black for the white kids and too white for the black kids – something I'm certain resonates with a lot of people. I went to a diverse, state secondary school and did my best to mirror my classmates in order to blend in. Education has always brought me joy. Armed with my bachelor's and master's degrees, I've recently embarked on my biggest challenge yet: the doctorate. However, the social side of education still remains a complete mystery to me.

In my first few months at secondary school I took a huge blow to my confidence, which was already hanging by a thread, as I ended up isolated from day one. I struggled to understand people's intentions, and although passive, I managed to get myself into numerous conflicts with classmates due to how much I struggled with my emotions. I felt as though everyone hated me or as if I was always in the wrong. It didn't really make sense to me as I couldn't understand why. Ensuring I wore the same clothes as my peers, scraping my naturally curly hair back into the tightest ponytail possible and slicking the edges down with Vaseline, I still didn't make any friends. I struggled in class as all I wanted to do was learn. The constant talking and general raucous behaviour was far too much to handle and I ended up just walking out of the classroom, to my own surprise. Anxiety and low self-esteem began to take over, starting to affect my relationships at home, too. I desperately wanted a group of friends, yet people never really understood me. I soon learned that I didn't understand them, either. I experienced many failed friendships, all of which ended with major bust-ups and misunderstandings. My hobbies were always too different or too academic, as was the way in which I spoke, expressed myself and communicated in general. I decided that instead of being excluded further, the best idea would be to stop communicating all together and shut myself away in my bubble. This became my safe space. I soon learned that by walking out of the classroom I'd be taken to isolation to do my work. It was a form of punishment for bad behaviour, but the thought of being able to decompress in a silent room brought nothing but relief. I now know that I wasn't badly behaved or troubled, but a child who was struggling to navigate a neurotypical world that posed so many challenges, all of which went completely unnoticed.

At the time, although I was unaware that it was a special interest of mine, reading became a form of escapism. It was the only time I could exist as my true self. I'd disappear into the pages, exploring my own world where, although isolated, I was protected. I remember my mum helping me to build a den in the garden using some old curtains and gardening supplies. I'd hide away whenever I could and devour book after book. It soon became my safe space, as I discovered a world in which I felt valid and grounded and it was the only way to escape the intense sensations of stress and anxiety evoked by the world beyond the pages. Reading gave me a sense of community and belonging, and I was drawn in by each word on the page. I guess it was therapeutic in many ways. I began reading science fiction and fantasy during secondary school and it soon became a world in which being the 'other' was welcomed. I identified with the alien protagonists, cyborgs and marginalized groups. They reflected my very existence. Literature has been safe space ever since and has become a way of dealing with my anxiety and a profound sense of being distanced from the world. There's something so calming about seeing the words on the page and identifying with all of them. I seldom identify with other people, so books and language are the ways in which I connect and understand. Since my diagnosis at the age of 26, I've come to realize that reading is essential for me. It's a basic necessity, like food or water. It helps me to regulate my emotions and thoughts and has played a key role in my self-acceptance. Literature has embraced me for many years and has kept me safe from a challenging and overwhelming outside world.

I've grown alongside literature and, regardless of external changes, it's constant. It makes me feel grounded and gives me a sense of being rooted in something: stability. It's where I belong. Regardless of whatever else changes, books and language will always be stable and comforting. I've come to learn that the way in which I identify with fictional characters is much more intense than the way I identify with real people. I've been told this is 'weird', many a time, or that I need to 'come back to the real world' – creating a sense of rejection that has definitely challenged my own well-being. I hope that, one day, autistic people will be accepted and perhaps even understood within this neurotypical world. Nobody understands what you're going through better than you do. Although there's still a significant way to go in terms of achieving equality and inclusion, autistic voices are being heard and will eventually be understood.

Pre-diagnosis was an incredibly challenging and confusing time for me and I'd pretty much given up on trying to be like everyone else. I decided I'd never fit in and I'd probably never have any friends. Since diagnosis and engaging with the online autism community, I feel incredibly validated and I've learned that trying to fit in is not the answer to finding joy and happiness. Reading experiences written by other autistic people and which mirrored my own experiences gave me hope, a sense of belonging and made me realize that channelling our strengths is just as important as receiving support in the areas we find more challenging. It's very easy to oversee your strengths, talents and abilities when you're struggling in other areas of your life. A sense of hope can vary from person from person, but YOU are that hope. Don't change for other people, change for yourself. Focus on building your sense of self as opposed to losing it to masking, imitating or trying to blend in. You're powerful, you're valid and no matter how long it takes, you'll find your niche in this world and you'll flourish.

# Conclusion

The topic of mental health often goes down the route of psychiatric diagnoses, and I'm sure that many of you readers picked up this book looking for information on specific diagnoses that you or your loved one have been given. I wanted to show, however, that, diagnosis or not, mental health is about the whole person and the world they live in. A sense of contentment and internal happiness does not simply come from curing a psychiatric disorder. Lasting and meaningful mental health comes from a deep sense of security, fulfilment and authenticity. A lack of security caused by a society that is not equal, fair or just, where basic needs are not met, is just as important in the mental health debate as medication. To have a sense of security and safety is the most basic part of mental health; it is the skeleton on which the body of mental health can be built. Until a person can feel secure and safe, they are not going to achieve meaningful mental health. For autistic people living in societies that do not give them a sense of security, the societies themselves are a fundamental barrier to health and happiness.

When people are stifled from achieving a sense of fulfilment because of systemic failings and discrimination, people's mental health suffers. Feeling as though we are meeting our full potential and achieving the things we want to achieve is how we gain a sense of purpose, meaning and motivation. These are key components to a healthy and happy life, the flesh, blood and organs of mental health. Many of the contributors outlined how education and employment systems were actively damaging. Fulfilment comes in many forms, and part of this is education and employment. However, if we cannot access these spaces, then our road to fulfilment is barricaded shut.

When people are forced to change who they are in order to fit into an intolerant society, internal and external shame will persist. We all deserve to live our lives as ourselves, to not feel terrible and heart aching shame about who we are. However, many autistic people are forced to live under these conditions. They are born into a world built on generations of shame around autism and disability, making it a hostile environment. Growing up and living in this hostile environment stifles any sense of pride in ourselves. Instead, internalized self-hatred, low self-esteem and low self-worth boil through our bodies. Authenticity is more than a faddy slogan to put on t-shirts; it is the beating heart of mental health.

These three components – security, fulfilment and authenticity – are the same for someone who is in the middle of a mental health crisis and someone who is going about their average day. We all need them, autistic or not. There are many ways we as individuals can help ourselves to achieve better security, fulfilment and authenticity. The contributors have outlined many skills and techniques that help them improve their mental health or change a difficult situation they were or are in. We are all responsible for our own health and we have the capacity to make decisions that can help or hinder us. Socio-economic factors play a large role in this, of course, but that does not mean we cannot also work to help ourselves.

Part of that may be to 'recover' from an illness. Take 'recovery' to mean whatever you believe it to be; there is no one single way or goal, your recovery is yours to define. The stories within this book have shown different mental health journeys, from dealing with suicidal thoughts, to managing anxiety day to day, to life with schizophrenia. What I hope comes across is that whatever it is you are going through right now, there is a way forward. I am sure that you may have seen or heard the phrase 'It will get better!' I am also sure it probably annoyed you; it certainly annoyed me when I was at my worst. But I'm afraid, they were right. I think the reason it annoyed me so much was because I couldn't see a way out, those words were far too abstract to take on board when I felt as if I was dying. What I needed was to know that others had been where I was and had survived: no, not just survived, but had gone on to be happy. I needed to see that there was a path out of that pain and despair. It didn't need to be clear. I didn't need someone to drag me down that path either. I just needed to know it was there, waiting for me when I was ready.

Whether you define your struggles as illness, distress, trauma, or whatever, in the thick of it all hope seems lost. I am here to be the annoying one who tells you that there is hope. You may not be ready to accept it, you may not be ready to believe me, but I will say it nonetheless. It is okay if you are not ready to accept it. For years I refused, consciously or unconsciously, to accept that there was hope. I felt as if I was protecting myself by disallowing this feeling. When I was ready to feel it, the fear never left, but I was in a position in which I could walk through that fear to reach a place where I was happy. I wish I could say there was one magical thing that made me ready to take this journey, but in reality there wasn't. All I can say is, you know it when you feel it – which is infuriatingly vague. The contributors have all shared their journeys to hopefulness; some are further than others down this path, but the thing most have in common is that they have all learned to accept themselves to a lesser or greater degree.

As individuals, we have all reflected on our place in the world also. It is near impossible to discuss mental health without also discussing how we fit into the world and how the world fits within us. All the contributors outlined their hope for a free, just, inclusive and accessible society. A world where those with any neurological difference can have a meaningful contribution in society, utilize their skills and reach their potential. A world that understands and fully accepts autistic people for who they are. A world where autistic children can grow up, be supported, and not experience trauma. A world where autism isn't defined by the distress we experience. A world that values difference.

I know how hard it is to feel that this is an achievable goal. I know what it is like to look at how the world is now and think a better future doesn't exist. I know the painful stab in the heart when neurodivergent people experience mistreatment. However, I sincerely believe that hope is not lost.

It is important to acknowledge and understand that autistic people all over the world are facing monstrous challenges. The societies we live in and the institutions within those societies are frequently inaccessible and often traumatizing. The emotional and psychological toll this takes can often be disabling. However, we must also recognize how far we have come.

*Homo sapiens* are problem-solvers, we are biological machines with brains that have evolved to have problem-solving abilities. This has led to the expansion of humans across the globe. Being problem-solvers is, of course, advantageous; however, it also means we are always on the search for the next problem. We can become feverish in our drive to always see problems. We find it harder to look back and recognize how much we have achieved. Neurodivergent people are excellent problem-solvers – the true engineers of innovation and forward thinking. I feel that we, as a group of people, may be far more inclined to perceive problems and overlook achievements. I am sure the complex interplay between our natural dispositions and the trauma and low self-esteem must play a role in this.

We now stand on the shoulders (not literally) of those who have spoken out, advocated and rebelled before us. The groundwork has been laid by the autistic elders. We now have the opportunity to live as part of society – an opportunity that those who came before us did not have. People do listen to us; more and more our voices are being heard. More and more our words are being read. Changes are being made. Some research groups are listening to us, including us, and researching the things that matter to us. Education, healthcare and employment institutions are starting to have crucial conversations which will pave a way to institutional change. Autistic voices are key to this change.

In contrast to my previous point regarding our problem-solving nature, this ability to solve problems is exactly why I think hope is not lost. The task of bringing about societal change may seem daunting but each problem solved is one step closer to our goal. The little victories eventually add up to something much greater. The world will not change overnight, but the world will change in our lifetimes. We are witness to great change. We are a part of this great change.

One thing that autistic people share is a sharp and powerful sense of justice. Where we see injustice, it hurts us down to our very core. Personally, much of the hurt I experience is down to witnessing injustice. People say to 'let it go', or 'it's not your problem', but my sense of justice is equivalent to my sense of sight – it is a fundamental part of how I perceive the world. Injustice to me is very personal, even if at first glance it has nothing to do with me. While this powerful sense of justice is often a cause of pain for autistic people, it is also why I have hope. This sense of justice drives autistic people to fight for the causes they are passionate about; take Greta Thunberg[57,58] as an example. We are given strength from our desire to see the world become a better place. If we take the meaning of hope to be a desire to see a better future, then our drive to fight for what is right is inherently an act of hope. This is an inbuilt drive of hopefulness. On the whole, the autistic people I have met have all been incredibly hopeful people, even if they don't recognize it within themselves. My hope for the autism community comes from the autistic people fighting small or large battles every day in order to make the world a little better. Justice is more than the 'big problems' in this world, it is also about the small threads which make up our lives. It is the ability to have control over one's story. It is the ability to wake up every day without shame. It is the ability to access education, employment, healthcare, housing without unnecessary stress. These threads are coming together slowly. I have no doubt that autistic people and their drive to see justice will push this forward.

I outlined in the introduction a 'journey' that autistic people go through. I hope that has become clearer in your mind having read the contributors' stories. Part of that journey is to own our narratives. I write this conclusion chapter in the wake of Sia's ableist, disrespectful and abusive film.[59,60] A classic case of a neurotypical thinking they understand autistic people without putting the proper and suitable research in and neglecting any meaningful engagement with autistic people. This is narrative theft. These stories are our stories to tell, we know how to tell them accurately and respectfully. When we are given the opportunity to own our narratives, we have the ability to make real and life-changing differences in how society views us. With the community growing in confidence, more people are paying attention to our stories. More are realizing that we have a right to tell our own stories. More are realizing that when an event occurs, such as the one involving Sia, it is not right.

I once again bring in Greta Thunberg[57,58] as an example of hope. Her actions have done many things, including inspiring a global movement of children and young people to demand climate justice. The most appropriate action for this book, however, is that Ms Thunberg has shown the world that we, as autistic people, have the ability to drive global change, to move entire communities of people to act, to stand up and fight for what is right and just. While I don't feel comfortable putting so much responsibility on a single young person (many autistic people fight alongside Ms Thunberg and have been equally influential), Ms Thunberg's public protest was more than just about climate justice. Intentional or not, the world was forced to recognize that autistic people had a voice, a way of cutting through the bullsh*t, and an honesty capable of bringing down the façade hiding ignorance, greed and corruption. The world also realized that we have a wicked sense of humour. Ms Thunberg showed the world the power of autistic people's sense of justice. The world realized that our stories have power when we are allowed to tell them.

Ms Thunberg is one person, but there are many of us all over the world fighting our own little battles, whether they be our own mental health battles or battles with societal problems. We are all influencing change in our own ways. The more connected we become the more our community grows in strength. The community has been a key driving force in this slow and steady change. Social media does have its faults, but it has given neurodivergent people the chance to connect to each other and form a community, the like of which has not existed before. As cheesy as it may sound, we are stronger together. As a community, we have the clout to encourage real change in the world. Together we have the ability to build each other up. The rifts that occur within our community, between us, I believe to be the side-effects of the trauma we have all endured. These rifts are avoidable if we work towards a society that does not traumatize us. The slow and steady burn of progressive change may seem incomprehensible but the work we do in our lifetimes will mean that the autistic people of the future can live their lives with health and happiness.

This 'work' does not have to be far-reaching activism or advocacy; simply by putting in the personal effort to accept and value our own lives is a powerful statement. You don't have to be learned in the social, philosophical and anthropological theory of autism to make a difference – to be frank, I get intimidated by the complexity of it all – and you don't need to be up there with the autistic academics in your understanding. The most influential thing an autistic person can do, in my opinion, is value who they are as an individual.

While I hesitate to call autism acceptance a panacea (calling anything a panacea rings alarm bells in my head), the pivotal component of an accessible and inclusive society is acceptance of difference. Without acceptance, there is no true accessibility or inclusion. Instead, there are simply tokenistic gestures, which is what we often see now. Acceptance is not just our responsibility as autistic individuals, it is also the responsibility of everyone in society. We can and should put in the work to break free of the ways in which we have been taught to view ourselves, but we should also be holding society accountable for the ways in which we are oppressed. True allies to the autism community need to do the same. I would also like to emphasize that mental health at a societal level will not come unless there is acceptance. We as individuals can do what we can to help ourselves and learn to value ourselves, but mental health is intimately tied into socio-economic factors. Therefore, until we have a society that accepts, accommodates and values difference, then I cannot see how we, as a society, will be mentally healthy. It is in all of our best interests to first understand our own prejudices, ignorances and privileges, and then work on diminishing them in order to be able to accept all people.

I find it difficult to conclude a book with such a wide remit. I am also under instruction to not make this book depressing. I feel it is important to have a frank and honest discussion about the challenges we face as autistic people, and how these challenges may affect our mental health. I am aware that these can be heavy and emotionally draining topics to discuss, which can leave people feeling low. However, hope is what drives us forward. Without hope we would not be able to address any of the injustices we face; without hope there would be no future. At the individual level, hope can be a daunting thing, almost too abstract to understand. At our darkest times, it can feel as if all hope is lost. It is not lost, however. The stories in this book show that we are capable and deserving of happiness. It may not be an easy road to tread, but the journey to happiness is waiting for us when we are ready to take the first step. Whatever darkness you are going through now, there is a way out. A way out which will bring you contentment, joy and peace. The contributors to this book have offered their insights into how they helped themselves, and I hope you have found something you can take away to try in your own life. Perhaps the most crucial thing you can do, above and beyond the practical skills and techniques you use, is to find who you truly are and value that person.

At the societal level, looking back shows us how far we have come. By looking back, we can see that the general trend in society is towards progressive change. This will not stop. Change is at hand, and within our lifetimes the world will learn to accept us. Our sense of justice and problem-solving abilities will be a driving force in this change. True change will come when we realize that all the battles we face in society, from ableism, to racism, to climate crisis, are one and the same thing, products of old and defunct ways of thinking. New thought, new generations are coming through and will replace these old ways. For every Sia there is a Greta. The societies of the future will be built on accessibility, inclusion and, above all else, acceptance. In the meantime, we keep taking steps forward; we win the small battles we all face every day; we pick ourselves up when we fall down; we hold those responsible accountable when we face barriers; and we value each other. I said this in the introduction, but I feel it would be right to end the book with it also: I want the world to understand that we are here; we are here hand flapping and fidgeting; we are here not making eye contact; we are here demanding justice.

# About the Authors

## Mair Elliott

Mair speaks and writes about her own personal experience of mental health care in the UK and being autistic. She works to change the way in which mental health services deliver care and treatment, particularly for young people. She is also studying marine biology at university and studying to become a Viniyoga teacher. Mair is an outdoor and nature enthusiast and can often be seen in her natural habitat, the coast of Wales.

## Morénike Giwa Onaiwu

Diagnosed as autistic in adulthood shortly after her children's autism diagnoses, Morénike is a global self-advocate, educator and disabled woman of colour in a neurodiverse, multicultural, serodifferent family. A prolific writer, public speaker and social scientist/activist whose work focuses on meaningful community involvement, human rights, justice and inclusion, Morénike is a Humanities Scholar at Rice University's Center for the Study of Women, Gender and Sexuality and a member of several executive boards. Publications include *Sincerely Your Autistic Child: What People on the Autism Spectrum Wish Their Parents Knew About Growing Up, Acceptance, and Identity* from Beacon Press and the forthcoming *Neurodiversity en Noir: A Collection of Black Neurodiverse Voices* from Jessica Kingsley Publishers.

## Paul Statham

Paul is originally from the Cotswolds, but now lives in South Devon with his wife. He has one daughter from a previous marriage. He currently works at a local supermarket part time, but has previously been a radar technician in the RAF and a retail store manager for several leading High Street names. He is also a writer and a YouTube vlogger.

## Suzy Rowland

Suzy Rowland is an author, autism and ADHD specialist trainer, cognitive behaviour therapist, and poet. She founded the #happyinschool project to foster well-being empowerment and change among parents and professionals, helping all participants to address and resolve the significant issues around educating neurodiverse youngsters. Her passion is to raise the bar for well-being for children in schools, particularly for autistic and ADHD children, using mindfulness, CBT, group work, storytelling and listening as her key tools. Her book *S.E.N.D. in the Clowns*, a handbook for parents of young people with autism and ADHD, was an Amazon bestseller in neurology. See www.suzyrowland.com for details.

## Emma Wishart

Emma was born in Brighton at the start of the 1970s, the younger of two daughters, to Victorian-valued parents. She loathed school and managed to escape an expensive education at the age of 16 with the bare minimum of qualifications, before embarking on a series of short-term, menial jobs in order to fund her insatiable music habit. She lived a traumatic and tumultuous life for 30 years before moving to Wales for a bit of peace and quiet, and ended up spending 12 years living in various inadequate temporary structures in the middle of a forest. She was diagnosed as autistic at the age of 45 when everything suddenly started to make sense, or at least the reasons why nothing made sense started to become clearer.

## Robert Joyce

Robert is a middle-aged male hoping to raise awareness and acceptance of autism through the telling of his personal story. Diagnosed late in life, he regularly writes and makes videos online on a wide range of topics relating to autism with a view to sharing his own understanding of living on the spectrum. He also enjoys being creative and sharing his love for his intense interests. These include Rubik's cubing, learning anything related to geometry, and the great outdoors.

## Nura Aabe

Nura has built on her personal experience of having a child with autism to found and help to run the community organization called Autism Independence. The organization supports marginalized families affected with autism. She has been pioneering raising awareness of autism in the black, ethnic, minority community. Nura is currently a PhD student at the University of Bristol and a TEDx speaker.

## Emma Cobb

Coming from an autism-rich family of all ages, Emma is a mum to autistic children, works in the field of autism, and was diagnosed at the age of 48. Emma lives in the East of England with her family, cats, collections and hobbies.

## Yenn Purkis

Yenn is an autistic and non-binary author, public speaker and community leader. They also have a diagnosis of schizophrenia. They are the author of eight published books on elements of autism and a regular blogger. Yenn is a public speaker with almost 20 years' experience and has presented at a range of events, including for TEDx Canberra in 2013.

## Casey Chonily

Casey loves to read, and watches too much TV, as it is an escape from their current reality, while helping to understand people's inner and outer selves. Casey deeply cares about animals and is concerned about climate change issues, to the point of great anxiety. Casey has a lovely family; sadly their nan recently got diagnosed with Alzheimer's, but she is still the special, wise empathetic heart of the family.

## Jess/Jai White

Jai is a neurodivergent translator and writer living in Granada, Spain. They are an avid reader and PhD student researching disruptions of dominant discourses of race and gender in Latin American and Caribbean speculative fiction. You'll find them exploring nature, engrossed in a book or writing in several languages.

# Endnotes

1    Elsabbagh, M., Divan, G., Koh, Y.J., Kim, Y.S. *et al.* (2012). 'Global prevalence of autism and other pervasive developmental disorders.' *Autism Research: Official Journal of the International Society for Autism Research*, 5(3), 160–179.

2    Singer, J. (1998). *Odd People In: The Birth of Community Amongst People on the Autistic Spectrum: A Personal Exploration of a New Social Movement Based on Neurological Diversity.* Sydney: Faculty of Humanities and Social Sciences, University of Technology, Sydney.

3    Bolton, P.F., Carcani-Rathwell, I., Hutton, J., Goode, S., Howlin, P. & Rutter, M. (2011). 'Epilepsy in autism: Features and correlates.' *British Journal of Psychiatry*, 198(4), 289–294.

4    Holingue, C., Newill, C., Lee, L.C., Pasricha, P.J. & Daniele Fallin, M. (2018). 'Gastrointestinal symptoms in autism spectrum disorder: A review of the literature on ascertainment and prevalence.' *Autism Research: Official Journal of the International Society for Autism Research*, 11(1), 24–36.

5    Cederlöf, M., Larsson, H., Lichtenstein, P., Almqvist, C., Serlachius, E. & Ludvigsson, J.F. (2016). 'Nationwide population-based cohort study of psychiatric disorders in individuals with Ehlers-Danlos syndrome or hypermobility syndrome and their siblings.' *BMC Psychiatry*, 16, 207.

6    Lever, A.G. & Geurts, H.M. (2016). 'Psychiatric co-occurring symptoms and disorders in young, middle-aged, and older adults with autism spectrum disorder.' *Journal of Autism and Developmental Disorders*, 46(6), 1916–1930.

7    Hollocks, M.J., Lerh, J.W., Magiati, I., Meiser-Stedman, R. & Brugha, T.S. (2018). 'Anxiety and depression in adults with autism spectrum disorder: A systematic review and meta-analysis.' *Psychological Medicine*, 49(4), 559–572.

8   Simonoff, E., Pickles, A., Charman, T., Chandler, S., Loucas, T. & Baird, G. (2008). 'Psychiatric disorders in children with autism spectrum disorders: Prevalence, comorbidity, and associated factors in a population-derived sample.' *Journal of the American Academy of Child and Adolescent Psychiatry*, 47(8), 921–929.

9   Westwood, H. & Tchanturia, K. (2017). 'Autism spectrum disorder in anorexia nervosa: An updated literature review.' *Current Psychiatry Reports*, 19(7), 41.

10  Meier, S.M., Petersen, L., Schendel, D.E., Mattheisen, M., Mortensen, P.B. & Mors, O. (2015). 'Obsessive-compulsive disorder and autism spectrum disorders: Longitudinal and offspring risk.' *PloS One*, 10(11), e0141703.

11  Rydén, G., Rydén, E. & Hetta, J. (2008). 'Borderline personality disorder and autism spectrum disorder in females: A cross-sectional study.' *Clinical Neuropsychiatry: Journal of Treatment Evaluation*, 5(1), 22–30.

12  Siebald, C., Khandaker, G.M., Zammit, S., Lewis, G. & Jones, P.B. (2016). 'Association between childhood psychiatric disorders and psychotic experiences in adolescence: A population-based longitudinal study.' *Comprehensive Psychiatry*, 69, 45–52.

13  Cross-Disorder Group of the Psychiatric Genomics Consortium (2013). 'Identification of risk loci with shared effects on five major psychiatric disorders: A genome-wide analysis.' *The Lancet*, 381, 1371–1379.

14  Goodall, C. (2018). '"I felt closed in and like I couldn't breathe": A qualitative study exploring the mainstream educational experiences of autistic young people.' *Autism & Developmental Language Impairments*, 3.

15  Humphrey, N. & Lewis, S. (2008). '"Make me normal": The views and experiences of pupils on the autistic spectrum in mainstream secondary schools.' *Autism*, 12(1), 23–46.

16  National Autistic Society (2016). *The autism employment gap*. National Autistic Society. Available at: www.autism.org.uk/what-we-do/news/government-must-tackle-the-autism-employment-gap [Accessed: 22/03/2021].

17  Barnard, J., Harvey, V., Potter, D. & Prior, A. (2001). *Ignored or Ineligible? The Reality of Adults with Autism Spectrum Disorders*. London: The National Autistic Society.

18  Calleja, S., Islam, F., Kingsley, J. & McDonald, R. (2020). 'Healthcare access for autistic adults: A systematic review.' *Medicine*, 99(29), e20899.

19  Bauminger, N. & Kasari, C. (2000). 'Loneliness and friendship in high-functioning children with autism.' *Child Development*, 71(2), 447–456.

20  Hirvikoski, T., Mittendorfer-Rutz, E., Boman, M., Larsson, H., Lichtenstein, P. & Bölte, S. (2016). 'Premature mortality in autism spectrum disorder.' *The British Journal of Psychiatry: The Journal of Mental Science*, 208(3), 232–238.

21  Autistica (2016). *Personal tragedies, public crisis.* Autistica. Available at: www.autistica.org.uk/about-us/reports-and-accounts [Accessed: 22/03/2021].

22  Rumball, F., Brook, L., Happé, F. & Karl, A. (2021). 'Heightened risk of posttraumatic stress disorder in adults with autism spectrum disorder: The role of cumulative trauma and memory deficits.' *Research in Developmental Disabilities*, 110, 103848.

23  Glover, G. & Olson, V. (2012). *Assessment and Treatment Units and Other Specialist Inpatient Care for People with Learning Disabilities in the Count-Me-In Surveys, 2006 to 2010.* Improving Health and Lives: Learning Disabilities Observatory.

24  Mayes, S.D., Gorman, A.A., Hillwig-Garcia, J. & Syed, E. (2013). 'Suicide ideation and attempts in children with autism.' *Research in Autism Spectrum Disorders*, 7(1), 109–119.

25  Hull, L., Petrides, K.V., Allison, C., Smith, P. *et al.* (2017). 'Putting on my best normal social camouflaging in adults with autism spectrum conditions.' *Journal of Autism and Developmental Disorders*, 47(8), 2519–2534.

26  Adamou, M., Johnson, M. & Alty, B. (2018). 'Autism Diagnostic Observation Schedule (ADOS) scores in males and females diagnosed with autism: A naturalistic study.' *Advances in Autism*, 4(2), 49–55.

27  Beggiato, A., Peyre, H., Maruani, A., Scheid, I. *et al.* (2017). 'Gender differences in autism spectrum disorders: Divergence among specific core symptoms.' *Autism Research: Official Journal of the International Society for Autism Research*, 10(4), 680–689.

28  Cassidy, S.A., Gould, K., Townsend, E., Pelton, M., Robertson, A.E. & Rodgers, J. (2020). 'Is camouflaging autistic traits associated with suicidal thoughts and behaviours? Expanding the interpersonal psychological

theory of suicide in an undergraduate student sample.' *Journal of Autism and Developmental Disorders*, 50(10), 3638–3648.

29  Mandell, D.S., Ittenbach, R.F., Levy, S.E. & Pinto-Martin, J.A. (2007). 'Disparities in diagnoses received prior to a diagnosis of autism spectrum disorder.' *Journal of Autism and Developmental Disorders*, 37(9), 1795–1802.

30  Mandell, D.S., Wiggins, L.D., Carpenter, L.A., Daniels, J. *et al.* (2009). 'Racial/ethnic disparities in the identification of children with autism spectrum disorders.' *American Journal of Public Health*, 99(3), 493–498.

31  Crenshaw, K. (1989). 'Demarginalizing the intersection of race and sex: A black feminist critique of antidiscrimination doctrine, feminist theory and antiracist politics.' *University of Chicago Legal Forum*, 1989(1).

32  Oxford English Dictionary (2021). 'intersectionality, n.' OED Online. Oxford University Press. Available at: www.oed.com/view/Entry/429843 [Accessed: 09/03/2021].

33  Lazarus, E. (1883). *An Epistle to the Hebrews*. New York, NY: The American Hebrew.

34  American Psychiatric Association (2013). *Diagnostic and Statistical Manual of Mental Disorders (DSM-5)*. Washington, DC: American Psychiatric Association.

35  Mead, S. (2014). *Intentional Peer Support: An Alternative Approach*. Bristol: Intentional Peer Support.

36  Rowland, S. (2020). *S.E.N.D. in the Clowns*. London: Hashtag Press.

37  Wu, N.S., Schairer, L.C., Dellor, E. & Grella, C. (2010). 'Childhood trauma and health outcomes in adults with comorbid substance abuse and mental health disorders.' *Addictive Behaviors*, 35(1), 68–71.

38  Smith, K. & Victor, C. (2019). 'Typologies of loneliness, living alone and social isolation, and their associations with physical and mental health.' *Ageing and Society*, 39(8), 1709–1730.

39  Zarit, S.H., Pearlin, L.I. & Schaie, K.W. (2018). *Care Giving Systems: Informal and Formal Helpers*. London and New York, NY: Routledge.

40  NICE (2017). *Autism spectrum disorder in under 19s: Recognition, referral and diagnosis. Clinical guideline [CG128]*. NICE. Available at: www.nice.org.uk/guidance/cg128 [Accessed: 22/03/2021].

41   Clare Ward, Special Networks. Available at: www.specialnetworks.co.uk [Accessed 22/03/2021].

42   The #happyinschool project is a forum for autism and ADHD parent advocacy, providing interactive training and empowerment programmes for parents, mental health professionals and educators, incorporating the cultural perspective of neurodiversity. Webpage: www.happyinschoolproject.com.

43   Knots Arts © Registered as a charity, Company no: 8631074.

44   National Autistic Society © Registered as a charity in England and Wales (269425) and in Scotland (SC039427).

45   Mindfulness in Schools Project © Registered as a charity in England and Wales (1168992).

46   Wing, L. (1996). *The Autistic Spectrum: A Guide for Parents and Professionals.* London: Constable.

47   Silberman, S. (2015). *NeuroTribes: The Legacy of Autism and the Future of Neurodiversity.* Sydney: Allen & Unwin.

48   Grandin, T. (1996). *Thinking in Pictures: And Other Reports from My Life with Autism.* New York, NY: Vintage Press.

49   National Autistic Society (2021). *Autistic people and inpatient mental health hospitals.* National Autistic Society. Available at: www.autism.org.uk/advice-and-guidance/topics/inpatient-mental-health-hospitals/autistic-people-and-inpatient-mental-health-hospit [Accessed: 22/03/2021]

50   Green, R.W. (1998). *The Explosive Child.* New York, NY: HarperCollins.

51   Wishart, E. (2020). *'But You Said...?!' A Story of Confusion Caused by Growing Up as an Undiagnosed Autistic Person.* [Kindle version.] Retrieved from www.amazon.com.

52   Fisher, J.M. (2012). *Fisher's Personal Transition Curve: Process of Personal Transition.* [Originally presented at the 10th International Personal Construct Congress, Berlin 1999.]

53   Rowe, A. (2018). *Asperger's Syndrome: Socialising & Social Energy: By the Girl with the Curly Hair.* London: Lonely Mind Books.

54 Sunflower lanyards are part of a scheme running in the UK where people with invisible and visible disabilities can wear a lanyard with a sunflower print which indicates to people and workers in shops/public spaces/public services that the person wearing the lanyard may need adjustments to access these spaces.

55 Rickwood, D. & Bussenschutt, G. (2015). 'Adult Step Up Step Down: A sub-acute short-term residential mental health service.' *International Journal of Psychosocial Rehabilitation*, 19(1), 13–21.

56 Milton, D.E.M. (2012). 'On the ontological status of autism: The "double empathy problem".' *Disability & Society*, 27(6), 883–887.

57 Thunberg, G. (2019). *No One Is Too Small to Make a Difference*. London: Penguin.

58 Ernman, M., Thunberg, G., Ernman, B. & Thunberg, S. (2021). *Our House is on Fire*. London: Penguin.

59 IMDb (2021). *Music: Review*. IMDb. Available at: www.imdb.com/title/tt7541720 [Accessed: 10/03/2021].

60 Hans, S. (2021). *Music review – Sia's tone-deaf treatment of autism*. The Guardian. Available at: www.theguardian.com/film/2021/feb/14/music-review-sias-tone-deaf-treatment-of-autism [Accessed: 10/03/2021].